Rediscovering Your New Life

A Guide on How to Experience God's Greater Blessings

E N JINOR

A Newness of Life Series, Ed. 1 Vol 1

For inquiries or requests, please contact the author at:
newnessoflifeseries@outlook.com

ISBN: 1987464133
ISBN-13: 978-1987464139

DEDICATION

I dedicate this book to God all mighty for His unending Love and Grace towards my family and I.

FOREWORD

E N Jinor operates in a unique gift of God that inspires, encourages and reaches out to the younger generation around the globe. The impact of the contents of this book will bless the lives of the entire body of Christ especially those in leadership and workers that revolutionize our ministries. I know this book is going to be used of God to edify the Church today. I believe this book will greatly help the Church. I thank God that E N Jinor allowed himself to be used by God in his particular call.

I recommend the teaching and inspiring words of God through this book.

--Bishop Michael and Herminia Cole
Vice President of International Missions and
Prelate of the North Dakota Jurisdiction
Church of God in Christ (COGIC)
North Dakota, USA

ENDORSEMENT

The writing style was easy to read especially for new believers to the Faith. The reader should have no problem with the message that was intended, especially the transition from the Old Covenant to the New Covenant. This book is recommended to every believer to get a better understanding for the change in covenants.

--Pastor Robert Smith
--Dr. Judy Fornara
Spiritual Life Church
MN, USA

SHORT SYNOPSIS

We all have asked the age old questions: "Why am I here?" and "How do I fulfill my purpose?" E N Jinor addresses these from a perspective of "Blessings" which we can only receive from God. It is not on our own, but by His creative power that we have gained our commission and destiny to be fulfilled while on earth. When we are Born Again, we receive New Life.

The biblical references and accounts in this book have been structured in such a way to help the reader gain a greater appreciation for one's purpose and destiny. We are challenged to think more deeply, we are encouraged and given a direction to help us navigate the journey of faith until we are taken to meet our Creator face-to-face.

I highly recommend this read. You will want to revisit it often.

--Elder Kim Moen
Church Administrator
Gospel Outreach Ministries
North Dakota Jurisdiction, USA

ACKNOWLEDGMENTS

I am thankful to my wife for her continuous support for my spiritual walk and ministry. I'd also like to acknowledge Bishop Michael and Herminia Cole for their mentorship and spiritual fatherhood.

I'd like to acknowledge Reverend George A Vegah, Pastor Tony Andrews, Pastor Robert Smith, Dr. Judy Fornara, Dr. Gregory Fondong, Elder Kim Moen, Minister Kaden Saley, Henry Mensa and Portia Mensa for their support and encouragement. Their wisdom and counsel played a significant role in the completion of this book.

Last but not least, I would like to say thank you to everyone who prayed for me, encouraged or helped me in one way or another, whose names are too many to be named here. May God richly reward you!

--E N Jinor
Fargo, ND USA

Unless otherwise mentioned, all scriptural quotations are taken from the New King James Version (NKJV) of the bible

INTRODUCTION

Everything you need to lead a fulfilled life is found in God's storehouse. Do you need healing, anointing for ministry, prosperity or career advancement? What about patience, joy, happiness, comfort, fulfillment, etc.? The world is full of sorrow and sadness, all sorts of uncertainties and depression so maybe all you need is assurance and love. How about just knowing God more and growing in His Grace?

Every good and perfect gift comes from the Father above and just like a good father blesses his child with gifts, it's God's good pleasure to give you every good thing. Why? Simply because He loves you immensely and wants you to enjoy every good gift found in His storehouse. Despite God's earnest desire to bless us however, many Christians fail to see His blessings manifest in their lives. In order to receive a gift, you first need to know the giver and understand how He gives; you need to have a relationship but a lot of people don't really know how to have a relationship with God. From the fall of Adam till now, God has dealt with human beings through the provisions of two covenants; The Old Covenant and the New Covenant. A proper understanding of the provisions of these covenants is important in receiving the greater blessings of God.

There are blessings and there are greater blessings. This book will walk you through the provisions of the covenants then will show you how to harness them to receive the greater blessings God has made available for you.

TABLE OF CONTENTS

CHAPTER ONE
BASICS OF THE COVENANTS

This chapter will introduce both the Old and New Covenants - their purpose and how they came about. Much of what is said in this chapter will be explained in greater detail in the proceeding chapters.

From creation until now, God's relationship with human beings has been based on two covenants – the Old Covenant which was established through Moses and the New Covenant, established through Jesus. In the beginning of creation, God made Adam and Eve in His own image. They were faultless, they were perfect. Then through Satan's deception, Adam sinned and became tarnished. Sin came into the world and all humanity became guilty (of sin) as a result[1]. There was a need for a remedy to restore Adam (humanity) back to a place of right standing and fellowship with God.

Consequence of Adam's Sin

When God made Adam and Eve, He gave them authority over all His creation to rule and have dominion over it[2]. The Hebrew word for "dominion" used here is "*Radah*" and it means to rule over, to reign, to subjugate. To reign means to hold royal office, like a king or queen. Basically, God gave rulership over His earthly creation to Adam which made him king and steward of God's earthly creation. When Adam and Eve sinned, they empowered the devil to use that authority to rule

---

[1] *Romans 5:14*
[2] *Genesis 1:26-28*

over the earth in their stead. God then drove Adam from the Garden of Eden and placed Cherubim[3] at the east of the garden and a flaming sword to guard the way to the tree of life[4].

When Adam sinned, his nature which was created in God's image and was once perfect became tarnished. As a result, all sorts of evil crept into the world such as death, sorrow, poverty, depression, sickness, hatred, separation from God, all sorts of sufferings and diseases, and the list goes on and on. Interestingly, driving Adam out of the Garden after he sinned to prevent him from eating of the tree of life was an act of love and mercy to humanity, not punishment. Imagine a world where the wicked could never die; a world where people were severely hurting from dreadful diseases yet they could not die but suffered for eternity; imagine a world where the strong and heartless continually oppressed the weak for eternity. This is what would have happened if Adam had eaten of the tree of life after he got stained by sin. Also, eating from the tree of life might have distorted God's plan of salvation through the death of Jesus on the cross since death would not have existed. Knowing this, God drove Adam out of the garden so he would not have access to the Tree of Life.

After Adam and Eve were driven from the Garden of Eden, God didn't cease to fellowship with them. Adam's sons, Abel and Cain still offered sacrifices to God and He still accepted Abel's sacrifice despite their fallen nature[5]. Shortly after Abel and Cain offered their sacrifices,

---

[3] winged angelic being (Ezekiel 1:5-28, Ezekiel 10)
[4] Genesis 3:24
[5] Genesis 4:1-15

Cain murdered his brother Abel out of envy and jealousy. God interrogated Cain, the first murderer that ever existed who murdered not just anybody but his own brother and he answered God without fear or remorse saying *"am I my brother's keeper?"* Throughout the Bible, whenever God spoke to human beings, they always trembled and were moved with fear and awe. But Cain had just committed murder yet he was freely, without fear or remorse, talking with God. Cain, though fallen (sinful) still had such an intimacy with God that it was like a "common thing" for God to talk with him. As the years went by, the nature of human beings grew so sinful that it became a way of life that had a great grip upon humanity. There was a need for salvation.

I have always asked myself why Jesus had to die to save us. God could have wiped out the entire human race and he could have created a new and better breed of humans. So why didn't He? Why did He have to make the Old Covenant and wait so many generations, even passing out judgement to many people along the way, then sacrificing Jesus just to save us when He could have just "fixed" Adam's blunder right from Genesis? Please read on to find out why.

God's Plan of Salvation

Now several generations later, God made a covenant with Abraham saying;

"And I will establish My covenant between Me and you *and your descendants after you in their generations, for an everlasting covenant, to be God to you and your descendants after you."*-Genesis 17:7.

Notice that this promise was futuristic. God said "I will establish my covenant with you...." Shortly after, God commanded Abraham to sacrifice Isaac and Abraham obeyed[6] (however, God did not allow him to kill Isaac). Right after Abraham proved his faith and devotion to God through his obedience to sacrifice Isaac, God established the covenant He had promised Abraham earlier in Genesis 17:7 saying:

"Then the Angel of the LORD called to Abraham **a second** *time out of heaven, and said:"* **By Myself I have sworn**, *says the LORD, because you have done this thing, and have not withheld your son, your only son -- blessing I will bless you, and multiplying I will multiply your descendants as the stars of the heaven and as the sand which is on the seashore; and your descendants shall possess the gate of their enemies.* **In your seed** *all the nations of the earth shall be blessed,* **because you have obeyed My voice**"-Genesis 22:15-18.

This was a fulfilment of the first covenant made in Genesis 17 but it was also at the same time, an establishment of an improved and separate covenant from that of Genesis 17. This second covenant was given to Abraham by promise in the sense that he did not have to do anything else for it to come to pass. Remember that in Genesis 17, the covenant was made between God and Abraham and Abraham had to fulfill his part of the covenant by keeping the terms of the covenant and circumcising all male children born throughout his lineage[7]. However, the separate covenant in Genesis 22 wasn't a covenant between God and Abraham. Rather, it was a covenant between God

---

[6] *Abraham's obedience had a significant bearing on the establishment of the New Covenant of Grace*
[7] *Genesis 17:9-14*

and Himself, given to Abraham by promise. This covenant demonstrates God's love and grace towards us. Although we all became guilty of sin through Adam's disobedience, God didn't obliterate the human race to recreate a new and improved breed of humans rather, He gave Abraham a promise of blessings and salvation. This covenant of promise is now manifested through Christ Jesus and every person who is born of the spirit of God can partake of this amazing promise. This is the New Covenant which extends to all peoples: Jews, Greeks and gentiles. That's why God told Abraham "in your seed (Christ), all the nations of the earth shall be blessed...."

Four hundred and thirty years later, God made another covenant with the people of Israel through Moses[8]. Unlike the first covenant made to Abraham that extended to all peoples, this covenant was restricted to or meant for the Jews and their households. It is also referred to as the Mosaic Covenant or the Old Covenant. It was based on self-righteousness through obedience of laws and regulations. Unlike the first covenant given to Abraham by promise, this covenant was made between God and Israel, through Moses. God's part of the covenant was to bless Israel and be their God and Israel's part was to honor God through keeping all His laws and regulations without fault.

Purpose of the Old Covenant

The bible says God does not change. However, it seems God dealt with people of the Old Covenant differently from the way He deals

---

[8] *Exodus 19-24; Exodus 34:10-28*

with us today; We don't see overt acts of God such as the earth literally opening up and swallowing people alive then supernaturally closing up like it did to Korah[9], or fire falling from heaven and burning sinners, or God speaking with a loud voice so everyone would hear, God appearing and showing His form to people, etc. In fact, Elijah called fire from heaven several times but Jesus rebuked His disciples who wanted to do the same thing. So, many people have a hard time reconciling this difference; did God change? The key to answering this question lies in understanding the purpose and provisions of the Old and New Covenants. God hated and punished sin then, and He still hates sin now. God held the children of Israel responsible for their sins then, but He held Jesus responsible for our sins now. On the cross, God unleashed His wrath on Jesus the same way He unleashed his anger on the children of Israel when they broke the laws.

The Old Covenant served as a 'work-in-progress' of the New Covenant made to Abraham by promise[10]. The Covenant promised to Abraham was futuristic and could not be materialized then because the hearts of the people were increasingly sinful, arrogant and proud so, they were not ready to walk in the promise. Matthew 7:6 says; *"Do not give what is holy to the dogs; nor cast your pearls before swine, lest they trample them under their feet, and turn and tear you in pieces."* 1Corinthians 2:14 says *"But the natural man does not receive the things of the Spirit of God, for they are foolishness to him; nor can he know them, because they are spiritually discerned."*

---

[9] *Numbers 16; Numbers 26:10*
[10] *Hebrews 10:1*

Human beings in the days of the patriarchs weren't ready to walk in the promise of the New Covenant; it would have been like giving a pearl to a swine or giving a holy thing to a dog. So, God established the Old Covenant to serve as a "work-in-progress" and as a tutor in order to bring humanity to a state where they could benefit from the Covenant of Promise.

Another reason for the Old Covenant was to "tame" the hearts of the Jews, because God had chosen them through Abraham[11] to manifest Jesus. Sin was increasing at an alarming rate and the hearts of the people became more and more evil to the extent that they became involved in human sacrifices, bestiality, sexual perversions, murder, anthropophagy, outright wickedness, etc. If God had done nothing, there might not have been a virgin left through whom Jesus would be born. Look at the state of the world at the time God sent the flood where there was none righteous except Noah; Sodom and Gomorrah where only Lot was righteous; even in Israel in Gibeah[12] where sodomy and sexual perversions seemed to be the norm. Before the law came, people although sinful compared themselves with one another and weighed their sins against each other. They thought they were righteous relative to each other. So, God brought the Old Covenant to break this mentality by introducing His standards and punishing or cursing anyone who defaulted. Obviously, no one could ever reach God's standards of righteousness through human efforts therefore,

---

[11] *1Kings 11:13, 32; 2Kings 21:7; Zachariah 3:2*
[12] *A city of the tribe of Benjamin, located just north of ancient Jerusalem - Judges 19*

their hearts were broken and they could see how much they needed God's intervention. So, the Law of Moses and the fear of punishment restrained the Jews and prevented them from being overly sinful. Although somewhat effective, the Law of Moses could not change their underlying nature of sin. It was like taming a lion; A Lion that is tamed in a zoo and fed so it doesn't need to hunt its own food cannot change into a goat. It may act friendly for a while but its nature can't be changed to that of a sheep. It's just a matter of time before it reverts to being a lion and starts killing its prey if the opportunity presents itself. Jeremiah 13:23 says *"Can a Cushite change his skin or a leopard its spots? Neither can you do good when doing evil comes so naturally."*-CEB

The Old Covenant is now obsolete[13] and was never intended to justify humankind towards God, neither was it intended to save humankind. Understanding and appropriating the provisions of God through Christ Jesus is what will give you rest in God[14] and enable you to experience the greater blessings of God.

---

[13] *Hebrews 8:13*
[14] *Hebrews 4:1-11*

CHAPTER TWO
THE OLD COVENANT

Why did God Almighty get into covenants with fallen and frail man? In this chapter, we will take a deeper look into the Old Covenant; the reasons for the covenant and how it fits into this dispensation of Grace.

When Adam sinned, God prepared a plan of salvation and promised to crush Satan through Jesus[1] and bring salvation to humanity[2]. The word covenant (*Hebrew: běriyth*) means an alliance, a pledge, formal agreement or contract between two or more parties that is binding on all parties involved. Many Christians live by the provisions of the Old Covenant without knowing it but what really is the Old Covenant all about? Is it merely some laws in the Old Testament that don't mean much in today's society? Does knowing about the Old Covenant even important or is it applicable today? Please read on to unveil the mystery of the Old Covenant in today's society.

God, After The Fall

As mentioned in Chapter One, when Adam sinned and was driven out of the garden, God didn't cease to fellowship with him. He continued to shower His mercies and love on Adam's household. An indication of this is seen in the story of Cain and Abel. Cain had just

---

[1] *Genesis 3:15*
[2] *Genesis 22:15-18*

murdered his brother Abel but did not show any remorse for doing so. When God asked him where Abel was, he responded without fear or seemliness as if murder was a normal thing to do. Ezekiel heard the voice of God and said it was like the sound of many waters[3]. God's presence alone talk-less of His voice commands some Godly awe and reverence even to an unbeliever. The children of Israel were so afraid of hearing directly from God that they asked Moses to do all the hearing from God on their behalf[4]. Yet, after committing a series of heinous crimes; envy, pride, jealousy, murder and lies, Cain did not feel any remorse but spoke arrogantly in the presence of God. He must have been so familiar with hearing God's voice however, because his spirit was dead or insensitive to God as a result of the fall of Adam, the fellowship he had with God did not very much change his heart. Romans 8:6-9 says;

"For to be carnally minded is death, but to be spiritually minded is life and peace. Because the carnal mind is enmity against God; for it is not subject to the law of God, nor indeed can be. So then, those who are in the flesh cannot please God...."

Since the hearts of the people were carnal, they could not be transformed even though God still talked with them so their hearts grew exceedingly in iniquity. For example, throughout the Old Testament God repeatedly performed countless miracles amidst the children of Israel but shortly after these miracles were performed, they

---

[3] *Ezekiel 43:2*
[4] *Exodus 20:18-21*

forgot about the power of God and went back to their old and sinful ways. That's why God repeatedly called them "stiff-necked[5]"; they never remembered all the mighty deeds God performed among them. No matter what God did, they could not be really, permanently transformed. In Mark 6, Jesus performed the miracle of multiplying 5 loaves and 2 fish to feed about 5000 men not counting women and children. So, there could be a total of well over 10000 people who got fed with 5 loaves and 2 fish. The disciples of Jesus saw this miracle but their hearts were too dull to understand the power of God. To them, it was like some kind of "trick". A few hours later, on the same day, they were terrified to see Jesus walking on water and they thought He was a ghost. The reason they were terrified was because they didn't believe in, or understand the power of God even though they had just witnessed it a few hours earlier. Their hearts, just like the people of the Old Covenant were hardened. Mark 6:52 says *"For they had not understood about the loaves, because their heart was hardened."*

When a person doesn't understand the mysteries of God, the devil comes and snatches away what was sown in their heart[6] but through the offering of Jesus, those who believe in Him have received a brand new heart and a new spirit[7] capable of understanding spiritual things.

There are several reasons why the hearts of humankind grew in sin apart from the fact that their hearts were dead (alienated) to God but one major reason was the fact that they did not have a revelation

---

[5] *Obstinate, stubbornly refusing to change one's opinion despite attempts to persuade one to do so -*
[6] *Matthew 13:18-19*
[7] *Ezekiel 36:26-27; 2Corinthians 5:17*

of who Satan really was. There is an African proverb that says *"if a son doesn't know what destroyed the father, what destroyed the father will also destroy the son."* Satan had beguiled Adam and Eve to sin and he was now ruling the minds and hearts of their descendants to do evil. They were slaves to sin and their hearts were ruled by Satan[8] but they did not really know who Satan, the root of their dilemma was so they remained in bondage.

Satan the Unknown

The word "Satan" occurs 54 times in the New King James Version of the Bible – 18 times in the Old Testament out of which 14 occurrences are in the book of Job (apart from the book of Job, there are only 4 occurrences of the word "Satan" in the old testament) whereas it occurs 36 times in the New Testament. The Word "demon" only appears 3 times in the Old Testament while it appears 67 times in the New Testament. The Pharisees called Satan Beelzebub which was an idol god of Ekron[9] because they did not really know who Satan was. Satan was sometimes referred in the Old Testament as the destroyer or the angel of death. In Daniel 10, the Angel of God referred to demonic beings as the Prince of Persia and Prince of Greece. Because Israel did not have an understanding of who Satan was, the Angel used an illustration or allegory to describe the demonic beings they were wrestling with so Daniel could understand. This is the same line of reasoning Apostle Paul used in 1Corinthians 3:1-3; the Christians in Corinth were carnally minded and could not understand the wisdom

---

[8] *Romans 6:16-17*
[9] *2Kings 1:2-3,16*

of God so he used an approach that a carnal person would understand. Jesus also used this method when He preached in parables. He used common, physical examples that His audience were familiar with to explain the things of God. In Matthew 13:11-15, the disciples of Jesus asked Him why He spoke to the Pharisees in parables. Jesus' answer was *"Because it has been given to you to know the mysteries of the kingdom of heaven, but to them it has not been given."* In other words, Jesus was saying "they can't understand the mysteries of the kingdom of heaven so I have to break-it down for them using stories about natural things so they can understand." The Message Bible Version puts it this way:

"You've been given insight into God's kingdom. You know how it works. Not everybody has this gift, this insight; it hasn't been given to them. Whenever someone has a ready heart for this, the insights and understandings flow freely. But if there is no readiness, any trace of receptivity soon disappears. That's why I tell stories: to create readiness, to nudge the people toward receptive insight. In their present state they can stare till doomsday and not see it, listen till they're blue in the face and not get it."-MSG

Deuteronomy 29:4 referring to the children of Israel says *"Yet the Lord has not given you a heart to perceive and eyes to see and ears to hear, to this very day."*

Jeremiah 5:21 says *"Hear this now, O foolish people, Without understanding, Who have eyes and see not, And who have ears and hear not..."*

Romans 11:8 says *"God has given them a spirit of stupor, Eyes that they should not see And ears that they should not hear, To this very day"*

Daniel as well as the mighty men of God in the Old Testament walked with God on a physical, canal basis, because they couldn't comprehend spiritual things[10]. The Angel just like Jesus and Apostle Paul, used a physical allegory to explain the spiritual reality of the demonic beings he was wrestling with. The Prince of Greece and Prince of Persia weren't literal human Princes; if that was the case, it wouldn't have taken both Angel Gabriel and Michael to defeat them and they won't have need of a struggle doing so. In Isaiah 37:36, it took just one Angel to kill over 185 thousand Assyrians in one night. Samson, David, his mighty men, Prophet Elijah, Prophet Samuel, etc. individually killed or incapacitated hundreds of soldiers in one go. It wouldn't have taken up to 2 powerful Angels to defeat the princes of Persia and Greece with much struggle if they were mere human princes.

Princes of Persia and Greece

The first dynasty of the kingdom of Persia, the Elamite Nation was formed through the unification of several fragmented small kingdoms[11]. They started as a small settlement but later grew so big. The borders of its territory stretched out from India to Egypt and Thrace including all Western Asia between the Black Sea, the Arabian Desert and the Indian Ocean. In fact, the territories of Persia extended through 127 nations[12]. Persia was the Kingdom that defeated the great kingdom of Babylon[13]. The Bible mentions that King Artaxertes, King

[10] Deuteronomy. 32:29; Isaiah 6:9-10; 42:19-20; Ezekiel 12:2; Matthew 13:14; Acts 28:26-27
[11] "Timeline History: A Journey Through Time." Persepolis, 12 Jun. 2017, www.persepolis.nu/timeline.htm.
[12] Esther 1:1-3
[13] Isaiah 13:17-18; Daniel 5:28

of Persia was called king of kings and their law could not be altered[14]. So, the Kingdom of Persia that started as small fragmented settlements had grown to become the world power at that time. This is descriptive of Satan; Angels of God are ministering spirits sent to serve servants of God[15] and Satan was an Angel of God before he sinned. Being an Angel, Satan was in the Garden of Eden as a servant, sent to minister to Adam but out of craftiness he grew from being a servant to a master and god of this world[16]. Ezekiel 28:13-14 talking about Satan says;

"You were in Eden, the garden of God; every precious stone was your covering: …. The workmanship of your timbrels and pipes was prepared for you on the day you were created. You were the anointed cherub who covers; I established you; You were on the holy mountain of God; You walked back and forth in the midst of fiery stones"

The New American Standard Bible Version puts it this way;

"You were in Eden, the garden of God… You were the anointed cherub who covers, ***And I placed you there****. You were on the holy mountain of God; You walked in the midst of the stones of fire…"*

Today's English Version puts it this way;

"You lived in Eden*, the garden of God, and wore gems of every kind: rubies and diamonds…."*

Hebrews 1 says ALL angels are ministering Spirits sent forth to serve those who will inherit salvation. So God placed Satan, a high

---

ranking Angel in the garden to serve Adam and Eve. Satan wasn't merely passing by when he tempted Eve; the bible says he lived in Eden, God put him there[17] to serve Adam and Eve. This shows how much love God has for us. He always gives His very best to us.

King Alexander the great, king of the kingdom of Ancient Greece later defeated the kingdom of Persia and became the world power in its stead. So, the angel used these great nations as an allegory to give Daniel a description of who Satan was. Although Daniel loved and trusted God on a physical level, he was spiritually alienated to God and couldn't comprehend deep spiritual mysteries like we do today through the Holy Spirit[18]. When Jesus died and resurrected, He gave us a brand new heart and a new spirit altogether[19] but prior to Jesus' resurrection, humankind had a fallen nature that was dead to God and couldn't understand spiritual mysteries[20].

In the Old Testament, Satan was also referred to as the Angel of death or the destroyer[21] because he had the power of death. The children of Israel saw Satan as God's angel of punishment and death so, they referred to him as Lord[22]. Although Satan had now become lord of this world, he wasn't God almighty but the children of Israel couldn't clearly differentiate between acts of God and acts of the devil. Let's take a look at a few examples;

---

[17] This is explained in much more details in book 2 of this Newness of Life series
[18] Colossians 1:26; 1 Corinthians 2:10; 1 Corinthians 2:6-16
[19] Ezekiel 36:26-27;
[20] Colossians 1:26; 1 Corinthians 2:10; 1 Corinthians 2:6-16
[21] Exodus. 12:23, Hebrews 11:28, Hebrews 2:14, Psalms 17:4, John. 10:10, 1 Corinthians 10:10; Revelations 9:11
[22] 1 Corinthians 10:10, 2 Sam. 24:15–16

In 1 Samuel 16:14, the bible says an evil spirit (*Hebrew: ra`*) from the lord tormented king soul. The New American Standard Bible puts it like this; *"...an evil spirit from the Lord terrorized him."* This gives an impression that God sent an evil spirit to terrorize King Saul but God is light, in him there's no darkness[23]. Let's take a look at a parallel example in the new testament. When Jesus cast out demons, the Pharisees accused him of casting demons using the power of the prince of demons but Jesus replied and said *"how can Satan cast out Satan? If a kingdom is divided against itself, that kingdom cannot stand* [24]*"* 1 Samuel 16:23 says *"whenever the spirit from God was upon Saul, that David would take a harp and play it with his hand. Then Saul would become refreshed and well, and the distressing spirit would depart from him."*

David was anointed of God so if he calmed an evil and distressing spirit that supposedly came from God almighty, is the kingdom of God divided against itself? A kingdom that is divided against itself cannot stand. In verse 30 of Mark 3, the Pharisees accused Jesus of having an evil spirit but Jesus said that was blasphemy against the Holy Spirit. Let's take a look at another example;

In 1kings 22, a lying spirit deceived the prophets and they prophesied falsely to king Ahab. Verse 23 says;

"Therefore look! The Lord has put a lying spirit in the mouth of all these prophets of yours, and the Lord has declared disaster against you."

Again, this gives an impression that the lying spirit came from God

---

23 *1John 1:5*
24 *Mark 3:22-30*

almighty but James 1:13 says God does not tempt anyone. Jesus said in John 8:44 that the devil is the father of lies and he (the devil) has nothing in Him[25] meaning He (Jesus) does not collaborate with the devil. You may have heard people say that God killed your loved ones, or afflicted you with a disease, or brought this pain or another in your life to teach you something, etc. but this is a deception, the same deception some of these great men of the Old Testament had to deal with. Exodus 12:23 says *"For the **LORD will pass through to strike the Egyptians**; and when He sees the blood on the lintel and on the two doorposts, the LORD will pass over the door and **not allow the destroyer to come into your houses to strike you.**"*

This gives an impression that the Lord will strike the Egyptians and at the same time will not allow the Destroyer to strike the Israelites. So, it would seem that the "Lord" who struck the Egyptians and the Destroyer were two different people but they are the same person who struck the Egyptians and was not permitted to strike Israel because of the blood on the door posts. Hebrews 11:28 says *"By faith he (Moses) kept the Passover and the sprinkling of blood, lest **he who destroyed the firstborn should touch them**"*. Hebrews 2:14 says the devil had the power of death. Revelations 9:11 says the Angel of the bottomless pit who was king of the locusts is called Abaddon in Hebrew or Apollyon in Greek. Both names mean Destroyer, Destroying Angel or The Destroying One.

Yet another example of a misrepresentation of Satan in the Old

---

[25] *John 14:30*

Testament can be seen in 2 Samuel 24:1. It says *"The Lord was angry at Israel again, and he made David think it would be a good idea to count the people in Israel and Judah"* -CEV

This scripture gives an impression that the Lord God incited David to conduct a census. Later we see that God was angry at David. So, why would He ask David to do a census just to be angry at him later for obeying? This exact story is narrated in 1 Chronicles 21. It says *"Now Satan stood up against Israel, and moved David to number Israel."* So, the author of 2 Samuel said the Lord moved David to do a census. Satan was indeed lord of the earth but he wasn't Lord Almighty. 1 Chronicles gives a better, more clear definition of who "lord" was in this case. It was Satan, not God almighty.

Going back to the example of Daniel, since the people of the Old Covenant didn't have a revelation of who Satan really was, the Angel used an allegory to describe the demonic forces they were fighting. Satan was now god and lord of this world (instead of Adam) so he had the legal right to execute judgement except to those who were protected through a covenant with God. The blood on the door posts was not meant to secure Israel from God's wrath but to secure them from Satan's.

A Matter of Legality

But God could have destroyed the entire human race and He could have recreated a better one; why did He have to go through all the trouble to the extent of sacrificing His begotten Son on the cross?

It was humiliating enough for Jesus to walk the earth in the body of a human. Just imagine the creator becoming like His creation. Philippians 2:7 says;

"…Christ Jesus, who, being in the form of God, did not consider it robbery to be equal with God, but made Himself of no reputation, taking the form of a bondservant, and coming in the likeness of men. And being found in appearance as a man, He humbled Himself and became obedient to the point of death, even the death of the cross."

Jesus was insulted, humiliated, reviled against, and killed by His own creation; He lost His reputation. Just imagine a parent who gave away so much time, money, efforts, everything to raise a child and then the child grows up and disowns the parent for no just reason. If you are a parent, you may relate with this example but Jesus suffered worse. It must have been so humiliating. The worst part is, Holy God who hates sin with every fiber of His being became the very definition of Sin (although He did not commit Sin) just so He could save us. An innocent God accused falsely, became Sin for us. At the garden of Gethsemane when Jesus cried, He wasn't crying because He was afraid to die. The apostles and early Christians were not afraid of death rather, they were happy and considered it a privilege, an honor to die for God. The apostles were not more courageous than Jesus so if they were not afraid to die for God, Jesus wasn't afraid to die for His father's work either. When He said "let this cup pass from me", He wasn't referring to the cup of death or suffering on the cross, rather he was referring to the cup of God's wrath as a result of Him becoming what He hates most - Sin. Isaiah 51:17 says;

"Awake, awake! Stand up, O Jerusalem, You who have drunk at the hand of the Lord The cup of His fury; You have drunk the dregs of the cup of trembling, And drained it out"

Holy Jesus was about to become Sin[26], what He hates the most and He would incur God's wrath on the cross as a result so He cried. While on the cross, God the father whom Jesus loved and kept talking about throughout His earthly ministry forsook (deserted, abandoned) Him[27]. This must have been a great humiliation for Jesus.

When a manufacturer produces a defective product, all they need to do is recycle it and create a better one. In Isaiah 64:8, Prophet Isaiah says *"But now, O Lord, You are our Father; We are the clay, and You our potter; And all we are the work of Your hand"*. In Jeremiah 18, God took Jeremiah to a potter's house and showed him a pot that was flawed. But the potter used clay to make another pot and God said in verse 6; *"O house of Israel, can I not do with you as this potter?" says the Lord. "Look, as the clay is in the potter's hand, so are you in My hand, O house of Israel!"* So, if God is able to destroy a faulty creation and create a better one that would not sin like Adam did, why didn't He? Why take a long route, letting Jesus go through all the pain and humiliation of being a rejected and pitiful mortal? The short answer is, it was a matter of legality. God had given Adam dominion over the earth and He had made him king and ruler of this earthly realm. So, God needed to make a covenant with

---

[26] *2 Corinthians 5:21*
[27] *Matthew 27:45-50*

Abraham and Moses, descendants of Adam in order to have a legal or jurisdictional right to intervene in Adam's kingdom. A king can't legally intervene in another's kingdom unless a covenant or agreement is made between both kingdoms. Let me explain:

In the beginning Almighty God, creator of heaven and earth[28], full of power, who has no one above Him and reports to no one, supreme and sovereign in every way made Adam, perfect and flawless. He then gave him dominion, authority over this world[29]. In other words, God made Adam ruler, king, and god of this world[30]. Psalm 115:16 says *"The heaven, even the heavens, are the Lord's;* **But the earth He has given to the children of men."** The earth was Adam's domain and it was Adam's responsibility to rule and have dominion over it. God being just, could not go back on His word because the gifts and callings of God are irrevocable[31]. Don't get this wrong, God is all powerful and He is subordinate to no one. He could have done anything He wanted, when He wanted, including taking back His gift of the earth from Adam. However, God has integrity. He abides by His word and He would not break His principle because He is a righteous God. In Psalm 89:34, God says *"My covenant I will not break, Nor alter the word that has gone out of My lips."* 1Samuel 15:29 says *"He who is the Glory of Israel does not lie or change his mind; for he is not a human being, that he should change his mind."* – NIV.

---

[28] *Psalm 146:6*
[29] *Genesis 1:26-30*
[30] *Psalm 82:6, John 10:34*
[31] *Romans 11:29, James 1:17*

Hebrews 1:3a says *"The Son is the radiance of God's glory and the exact representation of his being, sustaining all things by his powerful word"*-NIV.

Malachi 3:6 says *"For I am the Lord, I do not change; Therefore you are not consumed, O sons of Jacob."*

The whole universe stands as a result of the integrity of God's word. If God should change or go back on His word, the universe would collapse. That's what these scriptures are saying. Even though God had the power of taking back His gift of the Earth from Adam, the integrity of His word constrained Him. It is reassuring to know that we serve a God whose word we can rely on, knowing that He never goes back on His word. Every word of man may fail; your doctor's report may change, your employer may go back on their word, your school may go back on their word, your investor, banker, family, friends, loved ones, people you trust may go back on their word, but God will NEVER go back on His word. We can rely on everything He says even if our lives depended on it. Amen!

God told Adam that the day he ate of the fruit of knowledge of good and evil, he would surely die but He didn't tell Adam He would revoke his rulership of the earth. So, although death came to the world through Adam's disobedience, annihilating Adam and creating a new race would have violated God's word because God's gift of rulership of this earth to Adam was unconditional. It was Adam's prerogative to rule this earth as he saw fit. So, in order for God to directly intervene, He had to make a covenant with the descendants of Adam (humankind) in order to have a jurisdictional right to directly interfere.

In Genesis 17, God made a covenant with Abraham to be God to him and his descendants. This covenant gave God the right to intervene and correct the harm that Adam had done through his disobedience. You may ask, but God destroyed the world with a flood, a covenant hadn't been made with humankind yet. So, if God didn't need a covenant to destroy the world, why would he need a covenant to destroy Adam? When Adam and Eve sinned, God cursed the serpent saying "*And I will put enmity between you and the woman, And between your seed and her Seed; He shall bruise your head, And you shall bruise His heel[2].*" This curse was also a promise of hope to Adam (humankind). So, when the world became very evil, God intervened just enough to secure or ensure the promise of His seed but He didn't destroy every human being. So when Adam sinned, he lost his rulership of this earth over to Satan and Satan became the new ruler in his stead. Romans 6:16 says;

"*Do you not know that to whom you present yourselves slaves to obey, you are that one's slaves whom you obey, whether of sin leading to death, or of obedience leading to righteousness?*"

2Corinthians 4:4a says "*Satan, who is the god of this world, has blinded the minds of those who don't believe.*"-NLT

But God never gave Satan rulership of this world; God never made Satan god of this world either. Satan was a servant in the Garden of Eden so where did he get his godship from? How did Satan become

---

[2] *Genesis 3:15*

god of God's earthly creation? This was Adam's authority that Satan stole through deception and betrayal. Through sin, Adam gave his authority to Satan and Satan hid behind that transferred right and could now legally do as he pleased in the earth[33]. Previously, Satan was an Angel of God, a servant. After his rebellion, he became an enemy of God so how could he have gone before God to accused Job? God is holy and He hates sin yet Satan, a former servant now a rebel, God's enemy could go before God and accuse Job and Peter because he was now the ruler of God's earthly realm. He held the seat or office of Adam so he could go before God's presence in that capacity. God wouldn't take that authority from Satan either because Adam willingly (though ignorantly) gave it up to him thereby making him (Satan) the rightful ruler of the earth. In Matthew 8:29 the demons responded to Jesus saying, *"What have we to do with You, Jesus, You Son of God?* **Have You come here to torment us before the time?"** They were the legal rulers of the earth and they were in a sense telling Jesus, "you can't torment us now, we still hold rulership of this earth, it's not yet time". Jesus never tormented any demon, he only cast them out from people why? They were still the rulers of this earth. Adam willingly gave Satan that right and God wouldn't torment Satan for it (not until Christ would fulfill his mission as a human). In Matthew 4:8-9, Satan asked Jesus to worship him and he will give Jesus all the kingdoms and glory of the earth. Jesus was now human, and His humanity was subject to Satan's domain. Jesus could have argued with Satan over earthly

---

[33] *This is explained in more details in the second book of this Newness of Life series*

authority matters but Satan was cunning, he was indeed the ruler of this earth and he wanted to trick Jesus into obeying him and sinning against God the say way he tricked Adam. Satan was aiming for divine authority. He'd gained Adam's authority now he wanted God's very own authority as well. That was his plan of taking over God's very own authority because if Jesus had obeyed Satan, He too would have lost his divine authority to Satan the same way Adam lost his but Jesus used a different approach. He didn't argue authority matters with Satan, He said He'll worship God only. Do you see the gravity of Adam's sin and why Satan deceived Adam? He was selfish and thought about himself and how he would benefit. He coveted Adam's authority and now he was targeting God's very own authority. He wanted to be like God[34] and the quickest way was to steal Adam's authority through deception[35].

If you are born again, God has given you the authority to enjoy His abundant blessings in this life. Through His death and resurrection, Jesus has restored us back to a place of authority, better than what Adam had. Satan has been defeated so he can no longer go before God's presence to accuse you the way he accused Job or Peter because Satan has been defeated. But every time you submit yourself to Sin or Satan's schemes, you are giving Satan a legal right to steal your authority and to dominate over you. Because Adam relinquished his authority to Satan, only his descendant, a fellow human being hence

---

[34] Isaiah 14; Ezekiel 28
[35] This concept is explained in greater detail in the second book in this Newness of Life series

legal heir could take it back but humankind in their frailty couldn't accomplish this task so Jesus had to come to earth in the form of a human to restore humankind back to a place of rulership.

1 John 3:8b says *"For this purpose the Son of God was manifested, that He might destroy the works of the devil."*

Hebrews 2:15 says *"Inasmuch then as the children have partaken of flesh and blood, He Himself likewise shared in the same, that through death He might destroy him who had the power of death, that is, the devil, and release those who through fear of death were all their lifetime subject to bondage."*

Jesus didn't only restore our authority but He also made of us a superior breed of being[36]. As a born again, you are superior to Adam. Jesus has made you a superior being. Amen!

In summary, coming to earth as a man would mean directly interfering with the affairs of this earthly realm so God needed to make a covenant with human beings in order to have that legal authority to interfere. That's one reason He made a covenant with Abraham, then Moses. He was preparing the path for Jesus. Although God had the power to destroy Adam and Satan right from Genesis, He didn't do so. He chose to stick to the integrity of His word.

A Need for a Covenant of Condemnation

Recall that Satan was now the god of this world and had the power of death, so he had the authority and power to destroy whomever he

---

[36] *1 Corinthians 15:45; 2Corinthians 5:17; John 7:38*

desired but God had made a covenant with Israel that shielded them from the power of Satan. So, when Israel stepped out of the covenant through sin and unbelief, they became exposed and Satan would afflict them. When they made atoning sacrifices, they were once again covered by the covenant and Satan didn't have authority over them, so the plaques would stop. (There are instances however, where God Himself punished the children of Israel for their disobedience and rebellion).

Therefore, since they were blinded and lacked discernment they could neither understand Spiritual truths nor the schemes of the devil. Consequently, sin increased under the devil's reign and people began to justify themselves by comparing their righteousness with one another. For example, Lamech the father of Noah, son of Methuselah killed a man for hurting and wounding him and to justify himself in this act, he said if Cain was avenged for killing a man then he shall also be avenged seventy fold[37]. What he meant was, his act of murder was more justified than Cain's because it was an act of revenge as opposed to Cain's that was an act of jealousy and envy. So, Lamech is saying here that if Cain is justified before God and will be avenged should anybody kill him, then he is more justified in his act. The Pharisees were also fond of comparing their righteousness with others. They had their own weaknesses but they preferred pointing out the weaknesses of others rather than dealing with their own issues[38]. Comparing ones

---

[37] *Genesis 4:23-24*
[38] *Luke 18:10-14, John 8:9, Matthew 7:1-5*

righteousness with others and thinking one is relatively good is foolish because our most righteous state is like a filthy rag before God[39]. Galatians 6:4-6 says; *"Don't compare yourself with others. Just look at your own work to see if you have done anything to be proud of. You must each accept the responsibilities that are yours."*-ERV

So, God decided to impose His standards on Israel by introducing the law through Moses to show them how sinful they were and that they could not be justified by comparing themselves with one another, but should turn to God who was able to save them.

Another reason for the Law of Moses was to put a restraint on the people of Israel so that sin and wickedness could be kept in check. If God allowed human beings in their state without a restraint, there probably would not have been a virgin left in Israel through whom Jesus was born. Humanity was really without control and at the mercy of the devil. It got so bad that God had to destroy the world with a flood where only Noah and his family were saved. Same thing with Sodom and Gomorrah where only Lot and his 2 daughters were saved. God had to introduce His extremely high standards to prove to Israel that they were rotten in sin and needed to be saved. Galatians 3: 19 says *"What purpose then does the law serve? It was added because of transgressions, till the Seed should come to whom the promise was made."* God also used punishment so that through fear (of punishment), they would maintain a level of righteousness until Christ could be born. This is why the ministry of Moses is referred to as the "Ministry of

---

[39] *Isaiah 64:6*

condemnation[40]", it was meant to condemn and not to justify. Since nobody could perfectly keep all the laws of Moses, the wrath of God was frequently manifested. For example the earth swallowed up Korah, Dothan and Abiram for being rebellious[41], a woman's thigh would get rotten and her belly would swell if guilty of adultery[42], etc.

Purpose of the Law of Moses

When Adam sinned, God said to him *"Cursed is the ground for your sake; in toil you shall eat of it All the days of your life.... In the sweat of your face you shall eat bread till you return to the ground..."* -Genesis 3:17-19. The NIV version puts it this way *"Cursed is the ground because of you..."*

The word 'Curse' in this passage (*Hebrew: Arar*) means to execrate, i.e. to put under a curse. What God said in other words was "because of your disobedience, the ground has been put under a curse[43]." As a result, the entire creation now subject to Satan rebelled against the original intent of God[44]. Interestingly when Cain killed Abel, God told him the same thing He'd told Adam when he sinned. God said to Cain *"when you till the ground, it shall no longer yield its fruit to you..."*- Genesis 4:12. The ground had already been cursed when Adam sinned. God merely reminded Cain of the consequences of Adam's sin. God wanted to make Cain know that sin will create an opening for the devil to come in and have lunch with him.

---

[40] *2Corinthians 3:7-11*
[41] *Numbers 16*
[42] *Numbers 15:14-22*
[43] *Adam's disobedience also had a negative impact on the entire creation and herbivores turned to carnivores, etc.*
[44] *Romans 8:19-22*

Abraham was considered righteous but when you look at his life through the lens of the law, he had several weaknesses; he got married to his step sister Sarah[45], he had intercourse with Hagar and bore Ishmael which was an act of unbelief in God's promise of giving him Isaac through his wife Sarah; he lied to Pharaoh, King of Egypt and Abimelech King of Gerar about Sarah being his sister. Although this was half true, he was motivated by fear and unbelief in God. It was selfish to put the integrity of his wife at stake in order to save his own head, and the list goes on. For all these weaknesses God never rebuked Abraham; rather He blessed him and called him righteous. Noah committed incest with his 2 daughters but God did not rebuke him. Moses being a Jew got married to a Midianite which was contrary to the law but God did not rebuke him, in fact God zealously defended his marriage. When the law came however, Moses who was the most humble person on earth in his days was rebuked and punished by God because of disobedience and he did not enter the promise land. The point I am making here is, it was never God's intent from the beginning to punish human beings for their sins or alienate Himself from us, but humanity now at the mercy of Satan continued to sin more and more. People were now comparing their actions against others in an attempt of justifying their acts of unrighteousness rather than repenting. Satan was now in control of the hearts of the people and if nothing was done, there wouldn't have been any reverence given to God on the earth. This almost happened when God destroyed the

---

[45] *Sarah was the daughter of Terah, Abraham's father but they had different mothers*

world with a flood where only Noah was righteous. Imagine only one righteous person in the whole world. Just think of the world becoming like Sodom and Gomorrah or Gibeah. Just imagine being accosted by all the people in your city, insisting on raping your kids and guests where not even law enforcement could help you. That was the state of these cities. If you think there's evil in the world today, there was much more evil and less restraint back then. The world was becoming unthinkably wicked because the devil was loose and unrestrained, he was the god and lord of this world and no one could challenge him. In order to execute His plan of salvation, God made a covenant with Moses which served as a work-in-progress and a tutor to pave the way for Jesus and the New Covenant of Grace.

The Law as a Work in Progress

When a manufacturer wants to produce a product that is complex and has many moving parts, they start with a conceptual framework; a blue print that shows what the finished product should look like as well as guidelines on how to produce it. When the manufacturing process begins, the manufacturer produces other pieces that may not be too valuable by themselves but when assembled together, add much value to the final product and make it more useful. For example, a computer manufacturer won't just mold the entire computer all at once. The engineers will first develop a blueprint; a conceptual design and algorithms, then they'll manufacture or acquire smaller individual parts like the motherboard, hard drives, RAM, processors, power supply unit, video and sound cards, mouse, keyboards, etc. Each individual piece may not have much value by itself but once assembled together, they form a super computer. The individual pieces are a work-in-progress of the finished product, the computer.

The covenant that God made with Abraham in Genesis 22 was a conceptual framework of the New Covenant but for this covenant to be an effective finished product, there had to be a work-in-progress to prepare the hearts of the children of Israel and make them ready to walk in the gift of Grace of the covenant. Prior to the New Covenant, the children of Israel were carnal and couldn't receive anything from God spiritually. A carnal[46] person cannot understand the things of God because they are spiritually discerned[47]. 2Corinthians 3:14 says; *"But **their minds were blinded**. For until this day the same veil remains unlifted in the reading of the Old Testament, **because the veil is taken away in Christ.**"*

Romans 11:25 says; *"For I do not desire, brethren that you should be ignorant of this mystery, lest you should be wise in your own opinion that **blindness in part has happened to Israel until the fullness of the Gentiles has come in.**"*

So, the children of Israel under the Old Covenant were carnal and undiscerning of spiritual things. They had a heart of stone[48] and spiritually blind to the things of God so they couldn't discern spiritual things of God. Their hearts couldn't be transformed, there was no

---

[46] *Carnality means relying on the natural course of things or the natural (human) 5 senses.*
[47] *1 Corinthians 2:14*
[48] *Ezekiel 36:26; Ezekiel 11:19*

spiritual cure for sin so when sin spread, the only remedy was to destroy or punish them. It was like treating cancer. If cancer affects a leg or arm, in order to prevent it from spreading and to save the entire body, the cancer infested limb may have to be amputated. In order to stop rottenness from spreading in a bag of tomatoes, a farmer will throw away the rotten tomatoes in order to preserve the good ones. This is the same thing God did through the law of Moses. God didn't find pleasure in punishing the children of Israel and He doesn't find pleasure in punishing you. In Ezekiel 18:23, God says; *"Do I have any pleasure at all that the wicked should die?" says the Lord God, "and not that he should turn from his ways and live?"* God didn't find pleasure in destroying those who rebelled or disobeyed His laws. However, since their hearts couldn't be transformed under the law, in order to save the whole body and preserve His people for the coming of the seed of Abraham, God had to amputate the bad seeds. He had to get rid of the rotten tomatoes. This is one reason why Prophet Elijah killed the prophets of Baal. They were too far gone and couldn't be saved. They were like cancer; a bad example for the nation of Israel and were turning the people against God through their rebellion. So, they had to be amputated. Witches had to die because the children of Israel neither had the spiritual insight nor the power to cast out demons – they saw Satan as an Angel of God and called him Lord. They were spiritually blind so God had to manifest himself in a physical way whenever He gave instructions to the prophets. It was quite common for God to speak audibly to the prophets in the Old Covenant and angels would appear physically and give them instructions because their spirits were dead to God so they couldn't receive the things of God spiritually. They could not receive the baptism of the Holy Spirit; the Spirit of God came upon them but never stayed in or indwelt them like He does to born again believers today. So when Daniel prayed, the Angel had to physically bring the answers to him. God had to physically speak (with an audible voice or in a dream or vision) with Abraham, Moses, Elijah, Samuel and all the prophets and judges of the Old Covenant. In Luke 9:54 however, James and John wanted to call down fire from heaven the same way Prophet Elijah did but Jesus rebuked them. There was no need to destroy the disobedient seeds anymore because through Jesus we can now have a new heart and a new spirit capable of discerning the things of God. We no longer need to kill witches because through Jesus we now have the insight and power to cast out demons and evil spirits. We no longer need to hear God's voice audibly (although occasionally He may still speak to us audibly) because His Spirit lives inside of us and we can now discern His voice spiritually. So, as part of His grand scheme of salvation, God established the Old Covenant as a work in progress in order to "weed out" the bad seeds and prepare the children of Israel for the New Covenant.

The Law as a Tutor

"But before faith came, we were kept under guard by the law, kept for the faith which would afterward be revealed. Therefore the law was our tutor to bring us to Christ, that we might be justified by faith. But after faith has come, we are no longer under a tutor"- Galatians 3:23-25.

This scripture is clear enough. The Law of Moses was like as a father bringing up a child. You don't need to train a child to sin because they are born with a sinful nature. Rather, you need to teach the child righteousness. It may not make sense telling a 1-year old that they'll go to hell if they did something wrong, or that God hates sin, etc. they don't yet have the mental ability to comprehend such things. They can't understand why you're making a great deal out of what they've done. Trying to reason with them on a mental level and telling them that God doesn't approve of sinful behavior can't prevent them from doing wrong. They may not even fully understand what sin is. However, if you threaten to flog the child if s/he continues to do whatever behavior you're trying to train him or her out of, the fear of being spanked or grounded or disciplined would refrain the child to a great extent from doing wrong things[49] not because s/he is afraid of hell but because of fear of being disciplined. But if the child is an adult, say 21 years old, you can't flog him/her anymore if they commit a wrongful deed because their mental ability is now fully developed and they can now choose for themselves good or evil. In fact, if you tried fighting them, you run the risk of getting beat-up yourself. You can tell them that stealing is a bad habit; God dislikes it and sin will give Satan an entry into their lives, or the cops will arrest them and they'll go to jail, or they'll not have any good friends, etc. At the age of 21, they have the mental ability to process information about God and benefits of being righteous. Though they are no longer afraid of being disciplined, their mental ability is now fully developed and they now

---

[49] *Proverbs 22:15; Proverbs 13:24*

have the ability of choosing between good and evil for themselves.

The hearts of the people of Israel were blind to God's love and Grace[50] so God used this same principle through the law to "tame" or tutor them. God wanted to make them know that they were not righteous in themselves[51] and they needed to be saved. So God used many laws to refrain them from being fully open to the devil's deception of sin and He tagged punishment should they disobey, the same way a parent uses discipline to correct their child and teach them morality. Galatians 3: 19 says *"What purpose then does the law serve? It was added because of transgressions, till the Seed should come to whom the promise was made."*

God's laws were burdensome and impossible to keep[52]. The 10 commandments were mere categories of commandments; these were expanded to hundreds of laws that had to be obeyed. For example, a man or woman who discharged semen or blood (menstruation for women) was considered unclean (same as sin) and needed a sacrifice for atonement. Even people who had any contact with the former were considered unclean. Farmers were not supposed to harvest every crop on their farm; they had to leave some crops for the poor and foreigner (your source of income or livelihood could be your "farm"); lepers were considered unclean although some of them were not the cause of their ailment; any man who wore garments that was made from a blend

---

[50] *Isaiah 6:10, Rom 1:21-32*
[51] *Romans 3:23*
[52] *Galatians 2:16*

of fabric (linen and wool) had broken the law[53]; a man who shaved the corners of his beard had sinned; anybody who ate any animal that had cloven hooves like pigs had broken the law; it was forbidden to eat an animal you didn't kill; think of all the fish and meats we buy from the local grocery store. Most people rarely buy or rear live chicken or cattle in order to kill before eating so a majority of us would be living constantly in sin according to the Old Covenant laws. Mixed cropping was against the law so it was forbidding to cultivate two or more kinds of plant on the same piece of farm such as corn and bean seeds[54]. They were only allowed to plant one kind of seed per piece of farm (consider a portfolio investment as a symbolic example of mixed cropping); and the list is inexhaustible. People born with birth defects were forbidden to offer sacrifices or serving in God's presence[55]. So according to the law, if you were physically handicapped or if you had any kind of defect or infirmity, you wouldn't have had any chance of being in God's presence or serving in His sanctuary. Thank God we are no longer under the dispensation of the Law. We can always boldly approach the throne of God and obtain mercy and grace without fear of punishment. This is really amazing!

You may say "it is clear that this dispensation and level of civilization makes the laws of Moses obsolete so how does this knowledge benefit a believer in this current generation?" Well you see, the Law of Moses is not merely a list of "DOs" and "DON'Ts" but

---

[53] *Deuteronomy 22:11*
[54] *Deuteronomy 22:9-10*
[55] *Leviticus 21:16-23*

also comprises of the purpose of the laws, the attitude that provoked the establishment of the laws and the behavior that arose because of the laws. In the Old Covenant, people had to merit or earn their blessings or curses. In other words, they had to, by their own efforts, earn God's approval and blessings. Although today, people would not isolate themselves if they menstruated, or be sent away from church if they were handicapped or sacrifice cattle when they sinned or do any of those things required by the Law of Moses, if they have a performance mentality or the attitude that was intended by the Old Covenant, they'll be working under the provisions of the Old Covenant. When you try to earn God's approval by your own efforts wherein you must do this or that so God would do this or that for you (quid pro quo), you have a performance mindset and you'd be putting yourself under the provisions of the Law of Moses. You'd be telling God, "bring it on; I can attain your standards by myself so bless me by my acts of righteousness." Apostle Paul in most of his epistles said we are justified before God by Grace not by works[56].

You don't need to sacrifice lambs to atone for your sins to be under the Old Covenant. When you say "God would bless me because I do righteous things" or "God will bless me because I pray, I fast, and I don't commit sinful deeds" or "God will not bless you because you live in sin or you don't pray", etc., you're still under the Old Covenant. That's simply what the Law was all about - earning God's favor through human efforts. Jesus constantly rebuked the Pharisees because

---

[56] *"works" means your deeds, the things you do*

they had this attitude.

The Law of Moses was a corrective measure used in the Old Covenant to make people try to keep God's standards and prevent them from freely giving in to the devil. When Jesus died on the cross, he made the Old Covenant obsolete[57]. We now live by a New Covenant not the Old. This may be hard to grasp because it goes against the way in which this world operates. In our physical world, students get rewarded for studying hard, employees get rewarded depending on how well they perform, even scholarships, grants or aids that are meant to be free awards are based on some type of performance. There's probably no human concept or institution that rewards everybody independent of what they do or who they are. So, the concept of Grace is hard to accept for a carnal person but God is calling us to a greater spiritual reality.

To put this chapter into perspective, remember that the purpose of this book is to show you how to experience God's greater blessings. This chapter explained what the law of Moses was about so now you know that you can't earn God's greater blessings by your goodness or acts of righteousness. God will not withhold His blessings from you because of your short comings either. If He did, you'd be under the provisions of the Law not under Grace.

Now a question lingers; If God loves and accepts us despite of what we do, why would we want to live holy or pray or do anything to

---

[57] *Hebrews 8:10-13; Hebrews 10:8-9*

please God? Please read on and get a biblical balance to this.

Scriptures For Further Reading

- ❖ Romans 3:19 – 23; Romans 4:13 – 16
- ❖ Galatians 3:10 – 13, Galatians chapter 19:1 – chapter 25
- ❖ 2 Corinthians 3:7 – 16,
- ❖ 1 Timothy 1:8 – 11,
- ❖ Hebrews 4:8 – 10

CHAPTER THREE
THE NEW COVENANT

We've seen from Chapter One that God established the framework of the New Covenant with Jesus through Abraham. In this chapter, we will take a scriptural look at what the New Covenant is all about, how it differs from the Old Covenant and how it can be applied to our everyday lives as we seek to experience the greater blessings of God.

Now, we've already established that the New Covenant was given to Abraham by promise but was actually covenanted between God the father and Jesus. Galatians 3:17-18 says;

*"And this I say, that the law, which was four hundred and thirty years later, cannot annul the covenant that was **confirmed before by God in Christ**, that it should make the promise of no effect. For if the inheritance is of the law, it is no longer of promise; but **God gave it to Abraham by promise**."*

Hebrews 5:5-6 says *"So also Christ did not glorify Himself to become High Priest, but it was He who said to Him: "You are My Son, Today I have begotten You." As He also says in another place: "You are a priest forever According to the order of Melchizedek".*

Hebrews 5 is saying that Melchizedek gave the office of High Priest to Jesus. It is however amazing that Jesus was not yet born (as a human) when He received this office of High Priest by the order of Melchizedek, the same way Levi was not yet born when he received his priesthood. He (Levi) gave tithes to Melchizedek through Abraham and received his priesthood although he was not yet born[1]. This is the same thing that happened in Genesis 22:14-18 when God gave the promise to Abraham; God was at the same time making a covenant with His seed (Jesus) although He was not yet born in the flesh.

Now, the Levitical Priesthood[2] could not redeem the people or perfect them towards God so Jesus had to become a more effective High Priest, not according to the order of Aaron but of a higher order, the order of Melchizedek[3]. Because there was a change in priesthood, the administration of the law had to be changed as well[4]. The Levitical Priesthood required that the people earn their blessings through keeping all the laws. Failure to fulfill all the requirements of the Law resulted in curses or punishment. The new Priesthood however, where Jesus has become the High Priest is founded on better promises[5]. The Law of Moses is now obsolete because there's been a change in priesthood so we no longer abide by the provisions of the Levitical Priesthood. Now, let's take a deeper dive!

Law of the Conscience (Law of Sin and Death)

When Adam and Eve ate of the tree of the knowledge of good and evil, they received in them the ability to discern good and evil. Suddenly, the first couple realized it was not appropriate to be naked.

---

[1] Hebrews 7:5-9

[2] The tribe of Levi were set apart as priests in Israel under the law of Moses and they were charged with various duties in the sanctuary and administration of the law of Moses (Exodus 40:12-15; Numbers 18; Deuteronomy 18:1; Exodus 28:1; Jeremiah 33;18;)

[3] Hebrews 7:11-28

[4] Hebrews 7:12

[5] Hebrews 8:6-7

For the first time, they felt ashamed. Something had changed, but what was it? This couple that once had fellowship with God suddenly saw themselves unfit to meet with God the way they were. They'd always been naked, but after eating the fruit of the knowledge of good and evil, their perception of who they were with respect to who God was, changed. The fruit of the knowledge of good and evil gave them a new ability – knowing good and evil. They now saw their weaknesses and frailty in light of God's perfection but they lacked the means of closing the gap so they felt guilt, inferiority, unworthiness and condemnation. A new law had just been birthed – the law of the conscience also known as the law of sin and death. This law made people see their weaknesses and sinfulness but it didn't give them the ability to change, so they felt condemned. God never told Adam and Eve that being naked was a shameful thing. God never taught them to hide if they felt ashamed. Satan never taught them either. But the law of the conscience automatically triggered these behaviors; they automatically gained this knowledge. Every person from birth can differentiate at varying levels between right and wrong, good and evil. A person may decide to shut up their conscience[6] and become hardened to sin to the point where it would no longer matter if they committed murder, theft, lies, etc. non-the-less, we were all born with an active conscience that tells us what is right and what isn't. This law also tells everybody that there is a God and gives us a tip of a need for salvation. Romans 1:20 says;

"There are things about God that people cannot see—his eternal power and

---

all that makes him God. But since the beginning of the world, those things have been easy for people to understand. They are made clear in what God has made. So people have no excuse for the evil they do."-ERV

Nobody is a born atheist but people can decide to silence this law and become hardened to it. For example, a person who knows tobacco is bad for their health and wants to stop smoking but can't may feel guilt. If these feelings persist, it may get to a point where they silence it and become hardened or immune in their minds with respect to whatever evil they aren't able or willing to stop doing.

Before God gave his laws through Moses, the Law of the Conscience was already at work so, people knew in a sense that they had an obligation towards God. For example, going back to Adam and Eve, when they ate of the fruit of the knowledge of good and evil, they hid from God because they were naked. But God never told them they were naked. In fact, when God came walking in the Garden and asked Adam and Eve where they were, Adam said they were naked and God said *"Who told you that you were naked?[7]..."* God never told Cain "thou shalt not commit murder" yet Cain was held accountable for the murder of his brother Abel. Through the law of the conscience, Cain knew that what he did was wrong. Same thing with Lamech who killed a man as an act of revenge. This law became even more active and strong through the Law of Moses[8] because it condemned anyone who fell short of God's requirements without giving them the power over

---

[7] *Genesis 3:11*
[8] *Romans 7:9*

Sin. Although a born again can now override this law through Christ Jesus, it is still active in those who have given an opportunity to the devil through their mind. The devil through the fallen nature will try to condemn you through your conscience but if you are born-again, the Holy Spirit activates a different law in you. Romans 8:1-2 says there is now no condemnation to those who are in Christ Jesus. The law of the conscience condemns, but thank Jesus that God doesn't condemn us despite our weaknesses. Rather, we are justified in Him through the finished works of Jesus. The law of the conscience, same as the Law of Moses makes unbelievers see their need for salvation. Jesus said *"if anyone hears my words and do not believe, I do not judge him, for I did not come to judge the world but to save the world.*[9]*"*

In John 5:45, Jesus says *"Do not think that I shall accuse you to the Father; there is one who accuses you—Moses, in whom you trust".*

Even though you may commit unrighteous deeds, God doesn't condemn or judge rather, He desires to save you. Although God doesn't judge the world now there'll be a time, another dispensation yet to come, where Jesus will return as the great judge[10] and God will judge the world but until then, God doesn't judge you, rather He bears with you patiently, hoping you'll turn to Him and fellowship with Him freely.

---

[9] *John 12:47*
[10] *2 Timothy 4:1; Hebrews 9:27-28; Matthew 25:31-46; Acts 10:42; John 12:48; 2Thessalonians 1:7-9*

Law of The Spirit of Life in Christ Jesus

As mentioned earlier, there is a better law that operates in a believer in Christ; it is called the law of the Spirit of Life in Christ Jesus which has set us free from the law of the conscience. This law doesn't condemn; it justifies and bears witness of the righteousness of Christ Jesus that now operates in us through Christ. When you fall short of God's standards, instead of feeling condemned, ashamed, scared or reluctant to fellowship with God, or entertaining feelings of rejection as if God cares less now that you've sinned, the law of the Spirit of Life justifies you through the righteousness of God in you. This law says "you are the righteousness of God in Christ[11]." Therefore, come boldly to the throne of grace that you may obtain mercy and find grace to help in time of need. Confess the word of God from your Spirit and say "I am the righteousness of God therefore I cannot dwell in sin, I am the fragrance of Christ, when I'm weak God's strength is made perfect in my weakness, sin shall not rule over me because it's not my nature." This would embolden you to fellowship with God in His throne of Grace at all times because God bears witness with you through your renewed conscience. Apostle Paul says in Romans 9:1 "*I am speaking the truth; I belong to Christ and I do not lie.* **My conscience, ruled by the Holy Spirit**, *also assures me that I am not lying"-TEV*

God does not condemn you through your conscience because He has made you the righteousness of God in Christ. Hebrews 12:24 says;

---

[11] *2 Corinthians 2:15; 2 Corinthians 5:19-21*

"To Jesus the Mediator of the New Covenant and to the blood of sprinkling that speaks better things than that of Abel." The blood of Abel speaks vengeance and restitution but the blood of Jesus speaks justification and redemption. So when you fall short of God's requirements, the Holy Spirit tells you through your renewed conscience "you have been made righteous by Jesus through His blood, you have been made strong and you are holy" and it stirs up in you a sense of love (of God) that would empower you to live righteously. The devil is the one who condemns and he tries to accuse us of sin. Satan is the accuser of the brethren[12] but God justifies[13] Amen! Romans 4:5 says God justifies the ungodly; not just the godly but also the ungodly. So, despite your shortcomings and sins, God still justifies you because Jesus died for the Sin of the world and if you are born again, you've accepted His gift. A carnal person would see this as a license to live in sin but it is not. It is on the contrary a "passport" to live a life of righteousness of God in Christ.

Humanity through the devil's deception has always abused the good things God created, but this doesn't negate the goodness of the things God made available for us all to enjoy. For example, the fact that people abuse medications doesn't make medications a bad thing. There are a few exceptions recorded in the New Testament after Christ's resurrection where God passed out immediate judgment on people on account of a sin they committed as in the case of Ananias and Sapphira[14], Saul who was later called Paul the Apostle who was

---

[12] *Revelations 12:10*
[13] *Romans 4:5; 8:33*
[14] *Acts 5:1-5*

temporarily struck with blindness on his way to Damascus because he persecuted the church and obstructed the gospel[15], Elymas the sorcerer who was struck with blindness for obstructing the gospel[16] and the case of Herod who was struck by an angel and he died a violent death because he was arrogant and saw himself as god but did not give glory to God[17]. If you study these scriptures further, you'd understand why God passed out these drastic judgements but that is outside the scope of this book. In Luke 9:51-56, James and John wanted to release fire from heaven to destroy a village of the Samaritans because they did not receive Jesus but Jesus rebuked them. It is bad enough to reject Jesus. Whenever a person sins, s/he is in a sense rejecting Jesus, s/he is insulting the spirit of Grace and the gift of salvation, yet Jesus rebuked his disciples for wanting to call down fire like Elijah did. In the Old Covenant era, prophet Elijah was allowed to release fire from heaven upon the prophets of Baal and the soldiers of King Ahaziah. But in the New Covenant, the grace and love of God abounds to overflowing. The blood of bulls of the Old Covenant could not cleanse the children of Israel from dead works but the blood of Jesus that was offered spotless for our redemption is more than enough to cleanse our conscience from dead works[18]. So, instead of having a sin consciousness that will revive in you guilt and condemnation, be conscious of the righteousness of Christ in you that will revive in you the Love of God that is able to make you attain to the fullness of

---

[15] *Acts 22:6*
[16] *Acts 13:8-11*
[17] *Acts 12:20-24*
[18] *Hebrews 9:12-14*

God[19].

Referring to the ministry of the Holy Spirit, Jesus said *"And when He has come, He will convict the world of sin, and of righteousness, and of judgment: of sin, because they do not believe in Me; of righteousness, because I go to My Father and you see Me no more; of judgment, because the ruler of this world is judged[20]."* Jesus is saying here that the Holy Spirit convicts the world of the sin of not believing in Jesus but He convicts a born again of the righteousness of Christ. He tells you Satan is judged and shouldn't have control over you. Be renewed therefore in your conscience, knowing that God justifies you not of sin or weakness but of the righteousness of Christ Jesus in you. Amen!

The Two Natures

The word Nature from the scriptural context of this book is defined as *"the basic or inherent features, qualities, or character of a person or thing or an inborn or hereditary characteristics as an influence on or determinant of personality"* -Oxford Dictionary.

The Old Nature (Old Man, Adamic Nature)

"that you put off, concerning your former conduct, the old man which grows corrupt according to the deceitful lusts." – Ephesians 4:22

Going back to Genesis when Adam sinned, his nature became tainted. As a result, every human being after Adam was born with a

---

[19] *Hebrews 10:1-2, Ephesians 3:19*
[20] *John 16:8-11*

tainted or fallen nature[21]. This fallen nature is what is known as the Old Nature sometimes referred to as the Adamic Nature or Old Man. King David records in Psalms 51:5 saying "*I was brought forth in iniquity and in sin my mother conceived me.*" The same way a child is conceived through the sperm of a man, so was this nature transferred from Adam to the entire human race. King David said as a baby still in his mother's womb, he was already a sinner because the sperm he came out of was already tainted.

Genesis 5:3 says "*And Adam lived one hundred and thirty years, and begot a son **in his own likeness, after his image**, and named him Seth*".

Seth was born in Adam's image and likeness, not in God's. Adam's image and likeness was now sinful and tarnished so it was no longer like God's. Every person born after Adam, was born in Adam's likeness, after his image. You don't need to teach a baby how to do wrong things. The baby just flows in it naturally because that's the nature s/he was born with. That is why a baby as young as a few months old would do little things they know isn't pleasing to their parents then they'll observe to see their parents' reaction. This nature of sin is alive in an unbeliever irrespective of how good s/he is. This is the reason why Jesus was not born of the sperm of Joseph.

In the culture of Israel before and during the days of Jesus on earth, a male child was valued high above a female child. A man's identity spawned from his father's. The females on the contrary were

---

[21] *Romans 5:17; Romans 3:23*

not given as much importance in genealogy which explains why Jacob's daughter Dinah[22] didn't partake with her brothers in their father's inheritance. The twelve sons of Jacob became the twelve tribes[23] of Israel but Jacob had thirteen children not twelve. This is also seen in the case of the daughters of Zelophehad in Numbers 27:1-7. Zelophehad had only daughters and according to the custom of Israel, they were not eligible to receive an inheritance in the lands that were being shared by Joshua. Zelophehad's daughters came to Moses and Joshua and requested that this law be lifted. Then God added an exemption clause to the law of sharing properties that a girl would only partake of the sharing of properties if her father had no sons.

Jesus, Son of Mary

So, according to the Jewish culture, Jesus should have been born through Joseph (from Joseph's sperm or as a seed of Joseph). Both Mary and Joseph were descendants of David[24] but according to the Jewish custom at the time, Joseph being a male should have received more importance in the lineage of the messiah but Jesus wasn't born through Joseph impregnating Mary. If Jesus had been born through Joseph's sperm, He would have been born after the image of Adam, with the sin nature in Him and that would have rendered His blood unfit for our redemption; He (Jesus) would have been a sinner from

---

[22] *Dinah was Leah's seventh child and only daughter, whom she bore to Jacob, (Genesis 30:21).*

[23] *The tribe of Levi wasn't counted as a tribe of Israel (Numbers 1:47-48) and Joseph was represented by his two sons (Joshua 14:4) so the 12 tribes of Israel consisted of the 10 sons of Jacob (not counting Levi and Joseph) and the two sons of Joseph who represented their father.*

[24] *Mary was a descendant of David through Nathan, a son of David while Joseph was a descendant of David through Jeconiah also referred to as Coniah or Jehoiachin, another son of David whom God cursed saying none of his offspring will sit on the throne of David (Matthew 1, Luke 3, Jeremiah 22:24-30)*

birth regardless of what He did or didn't do. So, the Holy Spirit had to translate Jesus into Mary's womb so He would escape the corruption of the Old Nature. Since Mary was a virgin, her womb had not been "corrupted" by the sperm of a man; It was "pure". The Pharisees did not know this however, or at least they didn't believe that Jesus was conceived of the Holy Spirit and not of Joseph that is why they referred to Him as the carpenter's son[25].

Let's go back to Genesis 2. When God formed Adam, He forbade him from eating of the fruit of the knowledge of good and evil and tasked him with the duty of tending the garden. At this time, Eve had not yet been formed to a physical, human existence. After Eve was formed however, the bible doesn't mention that God commanded Eve not to eat of the forbidden fruit as well. In 1Corinthians 14:35, Apostle Paul urges husbands to teach their wives at home so, it's likely that Adam taught Eve the ways of God and told her not to eat of the fruit but God didn't personally command her not to. So, it was easier for the devil to tempt Eve because she'd received a "second hand" information about God's instructions concerning the fruit. 1Timothy 2:14 says *"And Adam was not deceived, but the woman being deceived, fell into transgression."* To be deceived means to believe something that is not true or to have a false impression of something but Adam knew the truth. God had personally given him instructions regarding the fruit so he wasn't deceived, he was fully aware of what he was doing when he ate the fruit. He knew fully well that he was sinning against God but

---

[25] *Joseph was a carpenter by trade*

because Eve didn't fully know the truth and because she'd not received direct instructions from God concerning the fruit, she was an easy target for the devil. So, when Eve ate of the fruit, she disobeyed Adam not God. After they'd sinned, the bible says in Genesis 3;

To the serpent, God said "**Because you have done this**, *you are cursed more than all cattle…*"

To Adam, God said "**Because you have heeded the voice of your wife, and have eaten from the tree of which I commanded you, saying, 'You shall not eat of it':** *"Cursed is the ground for your sake…"*

Now to Eve, God said *"I will greatly multiply your sorrow and your conception; In pain you shall bring forth children; Your desire shall be for your husband, And he shall rule over you."*

God gave a reason and consequence for the curse when He spoke to Adam because Adam directly violated the command of God. But to Eve, God didn't say "Because you disobeyed me…" or "because you heeded the voice of the serpent…." God didn't mention a cause for the curse but He informed Eve of the consequences of her sin. In other words, God said to Eve "since man (Adam) has now been corrupted, he will rule over you and because you were made for man (Adam), your desires shall continue to be for him even though he rules over you." It's like a wife who makes her husband drink to stupor then he loses control and beats her up. I would say, "Your husband shall beat you up because he's drunk" but this isn't a curse. It's merely saying "since you've intoxicated your husband, he will become violent towards you because he's not sober, he's under the influence of alcohol that you made him drink". Adam was now under Satan's influence because he ate the fruit that Eve gave him. Interestingly, God didn't drive Eve from the Garden. Here's what the bible says in Gen 3:22-24;

*"Behold, **the man** has become like one of Us, to know good and evil. And now, **lest he put out his hand** and take also of the tree of life, and eat, and live forever"- therefore **the Lord God sent him** out of the garden of Eden to till the ground from which **he** was taken. **So He drove out the man;** and He placed cherubim at the east of the Garden of Eden, and a flaming sword which turned every way, to guard the way to the tree of life."*

The Hebrew word for "man" used in Genesis 3:22 is transliterated "Adam", the male man Adam. Also notice the usage of a definite article "the" and singular pronouns "he, his" when referring to "man". God drove Adam not Eve. Eve could have remained in the Garden if she chose to but she went along with her husband Adam. Remember God said to Eve earlier in the same scripture: *"Your desire shall be for your husband, and he shall rule over you."* So, she followed her husband because her desire was for him and also because she was now one with him. In 1Corinthians 11:7-9, Apostle Paul says;

"For a man indeed ought not to cover his head, since he is the image and glory of God; but woman is the glory of man. For man is not from woman, but woman from man. Nor was man created for the woman, but woman for the man."

Paul is saying here that Eve was the glory of Adam and she was made for him not the other way around. Her purpose could only be fulfilled in Adam. So, although God didn't drive Eve out of the garden, she had to follow her husband. Eve, being the glory of Adam didn't sin against God but her iniquity was against Adam. Hosea 6:7 says *"But like Adam, you broke my covenant and betrayed my trust."*-NLT.

1Corinthians 15:22 says *"For as in Adam all die, even so in Christ all shall be made alive."*

Rom 5:12 says *"Therefore, just as **through one man sin entered the world**, and death through sin, and thus death **spread to all men…**"* The bible repeatedly holds the male Adam responsible for bringing Sin into the world but both Adam and Eve sinned. So, why does this scripture say "through one man?" – Because only one man (Adam) sinned against God which led to the corruption of the human nature.

Adam being the carrier of the fallen nature[26], passed it down to his descendants[27] through his semen. If it was possible to bring a human being to existence without being conceived from the sperm of a man, then the child would be perfect and without the Sin nature, just like Jesus was. However, Jesus (apart from Adam) is the only one who wasn't formed from the sperm of a man. This is why all humans are born sinners. Recall that a sinner is not defined merely by what s/he does but by who s/he is – his or her inherent nature. Good deeds alone cannot make a person righteous same as sinful deeds alone cannot make a person a sinner.

---

[26] *Old Nature or Old Man*
[27] *We are all Adam's descendants*

The Old Nature is like a tree that produces sin. The blood of the Old Covenant (of bulls and lambs) only covered for the fruits produced by this sin producing tree but could not pluck out the tree from its roots. God says in Isaiah 1:11; *"To what purpose is the multitude of your sacrifices to Me "Says the LORD." I have had enough of burnt offerings of rams and the fat of fed cattle. I do not delight in the blood of bulls, Or of lambs or goats".* The more they sacrificed, the more sin multiplied. Hebrews 10:3 says *"…in those sacrifices there is a reminder of sins every year."* It's like pruning a tree so it can bear even much more fruit. So, the more they sacrificed, the more sin increased.

The New Nature (New Man)

"and that you put on the new man which was created according to God, in true righteousness and holiness." -Ephesians 4:24

As opposed to the Old Nature, the New Nature is like a tree that produces righteousness[28]. When you become born again, God replaces your Old Nature with the New Nature[29]. That's what the bible means by "you are now a new creature". A person who isn't born again has a sinful nature, not because of the individual acts of sin they committed but because as a seed of Adam, their Old Nature hasn't been dealt with. At the new birth experience, God destroys the nature of sin[30] and replaces it with His Life that produces the New Nature[31]. Interestingly, whether you are righteous or sinful in the eyes of God depends on

---

[28] *Isaiah 61:3*
[29] *Ezekiel 36:26*
[30] *Romans 6:6*
[31] *2Corinthians 5:17, Romans 5:17*

your inherent nature; the Old or the New.

John 1:29 says; *"...Behold! The Lamb of God who takes away the sin of the world!"*

Note that the word sin in this scripture is singular not plural. The Greek word for sin used in this scripture is transliterated *"hamartia"* and it means a brand of sin that emphasizes it's self-originated or self-empowered nature. This is not referring to the individual acts of sin like covetousness, immorality, etc. This is talking about the source, the Nature of Sin which was formed as a result of Adam's disobedience. In contrast, Titus 2:14 says *"He gave his life to free us from **every kind of sin**, to cleanse us, and to make us his very own people, totally committed to doing good deeds"* –NLT. The Greek word for "sin" in this scripture is transliterated *"anomia"* and it means lawlessness, iniquity, contempt and violation of God's law. This is referring to the individual acts of sin. Good news is, Christ has paid for all sins, be-it the Nature of Sin itself or the individual acts of sin.

1John 2:2 says *"And He Himself is the propitiation for our sins, and not for ours only but also for the whole world."*

The word propitiation (atoning sacrifice) means to appease; to make an offering to appease (satisfy) an angry, offended party. If an unbeliever dies, s/he will go to hell not because of the individual acts of sin s/he committed (since Christ has already made an appeasing sacrifice for the whole world) but because s/he has rejected (failed to accept) Christ's offering of salvation. In other words, their Old Nature (which is what makes a person a sinner and therefore, responsible for individual acts of sin) has not been dealt with through accepting the lordship of Jesus in his/her life. In John 16:8-9, Jesus instructing His disciples concerning the Holy Spirit says;

"And when He has come, He will convict the world of sin, and of righteousness, and of judgment: **of sin, because they do not believe in Me***."*

The New Living Translation puts it this way;

"And when he comes, he will convict the world of its sin, and of God's righteousness, and of the coming judgment. **The world's sin is that it refuses to believe in me.***"*

Jesus has already paid for the Sin of the world, every body's sin (believers and unbelievers alike) has been paid for. Jesus is saying here that the world's sin is that it refuses to believe in Him; It refuses His gift of salvation. In the same manner, a believer will go to heaven not because s/he did righteous things (otherwise some unbelievers would be equally if not, more qualified for heaven than some believers and Christ would have died in vain), but because s/he has been reborn and now has the New Nature that makes him/her righteous. I'm I saying it doesn't matter what a person does as long as they've accepted Jesus? No! There's a valid reason why you should not live in Sin but should live righteously and fellowship with God. It's very important to get a balance to this teaching so please read on to uncover a biblical balance to what I am saying.

The New Covenant

For He has not despised nor abhorred the affliction of the afflicted; nor has He hidden His face from Him; But **when He cried to Him, He heard.** *My praise shall be of You in the great assembly;* **I will pay My vows before those who fear Him** - Ps 22:22-25.

Surety of the New Covenant

Contrary to the Old Covenant where God made a covenant with Israel through Moses and they had to earn God's blessings by their own efforts, under the New Covenant God the father made a covenant with Jesus because humanity being frail could not keep its end of the bargain of an eternal covenant with God[32]. Psalm 22, talking about Jesus says He will pay His vows. What He is saying here can be rephrased like this; "God the Father, I vow (enter into a covenant with you) that I will give my blood and receive the world's punishment so they can be redeemed (of their sinful nature) and be saved." Hebrews 7:22 says "*By so much more* **Jesus has become a surety of a better covenant**".

What does the word "surety" mean and who is a Surety? The Oxford dictionary defines a surety as;

"A person who takes responsibility for another's performance of an undertaking, for example their appearing in court or paying a debt."

If you go to a bank to get a loan but you aren't credit worthy or you

---

[32] *See Psalms 22; 22-25; Isaiah 53, Isaiah 42:1-7, Isaiah 61:1-3*

don't have enough collateral, the bank will ask you for a surety; somebody who has enough collateral, who is credit worthy and is willing to take responsibility for your loan. So, if you aren't able to pay off your debts, the bank will come after the surety. The surety serves as a guarantor to the bank that the loan will be repaid. Jesus is the Surety of the New Covenant; all the requirements of the New Covenant rest on Him, not you. When you fail to meet God's standards, He goes after Jesus not you and the good news is Jesus has already fulfilled God's requirements that is why under the New Covenant, unlike the Old Covenant, God doesn't impute your shortcomings on you[33]. 2 Corinthians 5:14 says;

"For the love of Christ compels us, because we judge thus: **that if One died for all, then all died;"**

Paul said in Galatians 2:20 *"I have been crucified with Christ…"* But Apostle Paul wasn't one of the 2 thieves on the cross when Christ was being crucified yet he says he's been crucified with Him. When Christ, our Surety incurred God's wrath on the cross and died for our sins, it was the same as us dying on the cross; our requirements towards God had been fulfilled. When your Surety pays off your loans, the bank stops coming after you even though the payment didn't originate from you. Every blessing you need from God, whether it is love, good health, peace, prosperity, acceptance, assurance, comfort, good relationships, the right connections, success, posterity, patience,

---

[33] *Psalm 32:2; Romans 4:6-9*

endurance, fellowship with God, anointing for ministry, protection… all the blessings you need, Jesus being the Surety of the New Covenant has already paid the requirements so you don't have to. When a person becomes born again, s/he is engrafted into Jesus not because s/he made a covenant of salvation but because s/he chose to partake of the covenant Jesus made with God the Father. Recall from Genesis 22:16-18 when God established the framework of the New Covenant, He said *"By Myself I have sworn, says the Lord… In your seed all the nations of the earth shall be blessed…."* Galatians 3:16 clarifies who the Seed of Abraham is. It says;

"Now to Abraham and his Seed were the promises made. He does not say, "And to seeds," as of many, but as of one, "And to your Seed," who is Christ."

Jesus, the Son of God is one with God the Father[34]. So, Genesis 22 says God swore by Himself that in the Seed of Abraham who is Jesus, the nations of the earth shall be blessed. Through the blood of Jesus, the sin producing nature is destroyed[35] and we receive a New Nature of righteousness[36]. So, we no longer do righteous deeds to be Holy or justified or approved rather because we have already been made Holy and accepted in the beloved. Jesus our Surety has already met the requirements on our behalf. Amen! Ephesians 2:8-10 says;

'For it is by God's grace that you have been saved through faith. It is not the result of your own efforts, but God's gift, so that no one can boast about it. God has made us what we are, and in our union with Christ Jesus he has created us for a life of good deeds,

---

[34] *John 10:30,*
[35] *Romans 6:6*
[36] *Ephesians 4:22-24; Colossians 3:9-11*

which he has already prepared for us to do" –TEV.

God loved us even when we were lost, deep in sin[37]. We needed salvation but could not save ourselves; God took it upon himself to die on our behalf and save us from the ensnare of the devil and the wrath of God. He took away the handwriting of requirements that was against us.[38] As our Surety, He paid our debts so we don't have to.

Saved by Grace

"Now to a laborer, his wages are not counted as a favor or a gift, but as an obligation (something owed to him). But to one who, not working [by the Law], trusts (believes fully) in Him Who justifies the ungodly, his faith is credited to him as righteousness (the standing acceptable to God). Thus David congratulates the man and pronounces a blessing on him to whom God credits righteousness apart from the works he does: Blessed and happy and to be envied are those whose iniquities are forgiven and whose sins are covered up and completely buried. Blessed and happy and to be envied is the person of **whose sin the Lord will take no account nor reckon it against him**"*-Romans 4:4-8 AMP.*

Apostle Paul is saying here that you were saved by Grace and God justifies you independent of your deeds. If you became holy by doing certain things, your salvation wouldn't be free anymore and God would have to reward or bless you as an obligatory payment for your acts of righteousness. In the same line of thought, God will have to curse and punish you every time you didn't fulfil your responsibilities.

---

[37] *John 3:16, Romans 5:7-8*
[38] *Colossians 2:14*

You can't experience God's greater blessings with this mindset because you will always fall short of your responsibilities towards God. James 2:10 says if you fail in only one responsibility towards God, you fail in all. You'd have to be 100 percent perfect, at all times. This is how the Law of Moses functioned; the people of the Old Covenant had to work for and deserve or earn their blessings and curses but we've been grafted into a better covenant of Grace where Jesus is the mediator and Surety. Amen! This does not mean that you should live in sin or not fellowship with God. If you think this way then you have not known the love of God and you don't know God. 1John 1:5-6 says *"God is light and in Him is no darkness at all. If we say that we have fellowship with Him, and walk in darkness, we lie and do not practice the truth."*

Titus 2:11-12 says *"For the grace of God that brings salvation has appeared to all men, teaching us that, denying ungodliness and worldly lusts, we should live soberly, righteously, and godly in the present age."*

It says the Grace of God teaches us to deny ungodliness. So, although you are already justified independent of the things you do, the Grace of God teaches you to live godly.

Galatians 2:20 says *"I have been crucified with Christ; it is no longer I who live, but Christ lives in me; and the life which I now live in the flesh I live by faith in the Son of God, who loved me and gave Himself for me"*.

So, the teaching of Grace doesn't encourage anyone to live in sin but it empowers you to live godly not through your ability but through God's strength in you. In the Old Covenant, emphasis was placed on sin, guilt and condemnation. In the New Covenant, emphasis is placed on the Righteousness of Christ (in you), Love and Grace of God.

Hebrews 10:22 says *"let us draw near with a true heart in full assurance of faith, having our hearts sprinkled from an evil conscience and our bodies washed with pure water"*.

Hebrews 9:14 says the blood of Christ purifies our consciences from dead works so we may serve the living God. Do you see the pattern here? God doesn't want you to be sin conscious. Grace makes you righteousness conscious so you can serve the living God. Sin consciousness makes guilt and condemnation come alive. It revives the law of the conscience in you which will hinder you from experiencing the fullness of God but the Grace of God creates in you a righteousness consciousness, not your human righteousness but the righteousness of God through Christ and He empowers you to live godly. The Law says "live holy so God will bless you", Grace says "live holy because you've already been accepted in the beloved and you are already blessed". As the Surety of the New Covenant, Jesus has finished the works that was expected for our righteousness on the cross, you no longer need to do religious deeds for God to accept or bless you[39]. Galatians 5:4 says;

"For if you are trying to make yourselves right with God by keeping the law, you have been cut off from Christ! You have fallen away from God's grace." –NLT.

It's like telling God, "I pray 10 hours a day, I read my Bible, I do not

---

[39] *Romans 3:24-28; Romans 5:15-21; Romans 11:5-6; Acts 13:39*

commit sin, I obey your word, I fast frequently, I evangelize often and win many souls to Christ, I live a godly life, etc. so God bless me, anoint me, etc." This may seem plausible but that is what the law was all about; earning God's blessings through your own deeds (the things you do for God). If that is your mentality concerning receiving from God then Galatians 5:4 says you are cut off from Christ and you have fallen from Grace. We can never merit God's approval by trying to meet His standards through our deeds. The prophets of old could not, you and I can't either. By the works of the law shall no flesh be justified[40]. Jesus is (and will ever be) the only person who fulfilled the law without fault so we won't have to.

As we've already seen in the previous chapter, the Law of Moses is not merely a list of things you should or should not do, but also the attitude of trying to earn God's acceptance, favor, blessings, etc. Although you may not sacrifice animal blood or abide by the specific things the Law of Moses demanded, as long as you have the mindset that God relates with you based on the things you do or do not do wherein you do religious things; you pray, you fast, you read your bible, etc. so God would bless you, or expect God to withhold his blessings from you or be angry at you because you did unrighteous deeds, you are under the law and cannot be justified despite your good works. Matthew 7:21-23 says that some will say they prophesied and did all sorts of good deeds in the name of the lord and God will still reject them. You are not justified by your deeds! The natural or religious

---

mind may find this hard to accept because it contradicts the physical course of things on earth wherein you get rewarded relative to your performance, but the ways of God aren't based on the natural course of things. True Christianity is based on the Word and Spirit of God. I had a conversation with a friend some time ago. At the time, She'd been born again for over 30 years and had been in ministry for more than 20 years. She is a preacher and God had blessed countless women through her but she still saw herself as a sinner. You see what the law will do to a person who lives by it? Why then did Jesus take over 33.5 years on earth to suffer and die a pitiful death on the cross if we could be saved by the law? If you say you are righteous by the things you do, you would be a liar because you will say "I am not perfect but just trying to be". To be justified through your deeds of righteousness, you must be 100 percent perfect in the flesh[41] (i.e. through your deeds). If you say "indeed I am 100 percent righteous and without any faults because I do not do wrong things", again you'd make the word of God a lie because Isaiah 64:6 says *"We are all infected and impure with sin.* **When we proudly display our righteous deeds, we find they are but filthy rags…"** –NLT. The Amplified Version puts it this way;

"For we have all become like one who is unclean [ceremonially, like a leper], **and all our righteousness (our best deeds of rightness and justice) is like filthy rags or a polluted garment;** *we all fade like a leaf, and our iniquities, like the wind…"* –AMP.

My friend had some weaknesses (we all do), so, she thought she was a

---

sinner although she had been born again and spirit filled for so long. This is what the Law of Moses and of the Conscience is all about – condemnation. But if you are born again, you've already been accepted through God's Grace[42] and God does not impute your sins unto you, that is why 1Corinthians 3:15 referring to a born again says if anyone's works (works of the flesh, sin) is burned, he will suffer loss but he himself shall be saved. The only instance where a born again dies and goes to hell is when s/he consciously (being fully aware of what s/he's doing) denies Jesus. This is a state of apostasy, a state beyond backsliding, a point of no return.

Hebrews 6:4-6 says *"For it is impossible for those who were once enlightened, and have tasted the heavenly gift, and have become partakers of the Holy Spirit, and have tasted the good word of God and the powers of the age to come, if they fall away, to renew them again to repentance, since they crucify again for themselves the Son of God, and put Him to an open shame."*

Let's take a closer look at what this scripture is saying about being apostate:

Have tasted of the heavenly gift and have partaken of the Holy Spirit; The word "partake" in this scripture comes from the Greek word *"Metochos"* and it means to share in the office, work and dignity, active partaker or partners with (the Holy Spirit). This is referring to believers who have actively partnered with the Holy Spirit; believers who have been deeply involved with the ministry of the Holy Spirit in

---

42 *Ephesians 1:5-7*

the work of God.

Have tasted the good word of God; the Greek word for "tasted" in this scripture is *"Geuomai"* and it means to experience absolutely (the word of God). These are believers who have had a great understanding and working knowledge of the word of God and have seen the word of God absolutely manifested (become physical and tangibly evident) in and through their lives.

Have tasted the powers of the age to come: Thirdly, they should have experienced (*Geuomai*) the powers of the age to come. The age to come is what is referred to in 2Corinthians 5 and also in 1Corinthians 15. Apostle Paul said *"For we know in part and we prophesy in part. But when that which is perfect has come, then that which is in part will be done away… now I know in part, but then I shall know just as I also am known[43]."* That which is perfect is our glorified bodies that we'll receive at the coming of Jesus and the resurrection of the saints. We will know all things because the mind of Christ in us will be fully manifested and the limitations of our current earthly human bodies won't be a factor anymore. We'll be perfect and won't be limited by our mortal bodies because we'll be clothed in our glorified bodies. Apostle Paul is saying here that to reach a state beyond saving, you should have experienced this power. This is referring to people who have deeply experienced the fullness of God. If such a person rejects Jesus after having such an awesome and unique experience, s/he can no longer be saved. It is within reason to believe this is why there can never be hope of salvation for Satan because he

---

[43] *1 Corinthians 13:9-12*

had once experienced God and walked in the greater power of God. God says in Hosea 14:4 *"I will heal their backsliding; I will love them freely, for My anger has turned away from him."* God, referring to the church in Ephesus says in Revelations 2:4 that they had lost their first love and asks them to repent. So Hebrews 6 is not referring to backsliding but a much worse state of intentional and conscious renunciation of God after fully knowing and experiencing His power.

The Law And Faith

"Yet the law is not of faith, but "the man who does them shall live by them[44]*"*

By dying on the cross, Jesus made the required payment on our behalf so we don't have to. Faith is relying on Jesus and hoping to benefit from what He's done. The Law on the other hand is relying on yourself, trusting your ability to please God and earning His blessings by the things you do. Romans 14:23 says everything that does not come from Faith is sin. So, living by the law is sin because the law is not of faith. Trusting your deeds and trying to earn God's blessings, is sin. Trying to live Holy or fast or pray or pay your tithes, etc. **BECAUSE** you want to earn God's blessings or because you are scared that if you don't do these things God will be angry at you, or He'll send the devourer to curse you, etc. is sin and you've fallen from Grace[45]. Don't get me wrong. Fasting, praying, giving, living Holy and all these things are good and God loves them but they will only count to your favor if you do them motivated by God's love and having faith in what He's

---

[44] *Leviticus 18:5; Galatians 3:12*
[45] *Galatians 5:4*

already done. You can't bribe God through your deeds. Galatians 3:12b says the person who does these things shall live by them. So, when you try to earn God's blessings through your deeds you are aligning yourself with the provisions of the Law of Moses and you would have to abide by all the requirements of the Levitical Priesthood including blood sacrifice for your atonement. On the other hand, when you believe in God and trust on the finished works of Jesus, you're aligning yourself with the provisions of the New Covenant of Grace and you'd have to abide by the requirements of the priesthood according to the order of Melchizedek where Jesus has become the High Priest. You can't mix both, it's either you live by the law or you live by Grace through faith. Jesus said in Mark 2:22 that no one pours new wine into old wineskins. In Deuteronomy 22:9, God forbade the children of Israel from sowing two different kinds of seed on the same piece of farm. James 1:7 says a double minded man should not expect to receive anything from God. What these scriptures are saying is, God loves order and you can't mix two opposing things. It's either Law or Grace. It's either you earn all your blessings including salvation through your own deeds or you have faith that Jesus has already earned them for you. It's either faith in God or no faith at all. The law is not of faith and anything that is not of faith is sin so quit trying to earn your blessings. Believe in God and seek to grow in His love.

Saved by Grace, Now What?

I have met Christians who are Grace extremists and don't see a need to pray, fast, live godly, etc. They say "If God loves and blesses us independently of what we do, what's the point trying to live holy or pray or fast or do all these things? What's there to prevent us from going wild and living ungodly and unrestrained lives?" This may be the same impression you're getting from reading this far but it's important to understand the balance of the teaching of Grace. I have already partly addressed these questions earlier-on in this chapter but I need to make an important biblical balance to the freedom we have received through Grace. Apostle Paul had a similar challenge when he taught the foundational truths of the Grace of God. His audience felt that he was encouraging sin which prompted him to ask the same question many Christians today ask. In Romans 6:1, Paul asks *"shall we continue in sin so that Grace may abound?"* Apostle Paul said in Hebrews 10:29 that if you sin willfully, you are insulting the spirit of Grace. As we've seen earlier, the Grace of God teaches you to live righteously but you have to believe in God. Grace only works by faith. God is a "gentleman" and He would not force anything on you including His Grace. Every blessing you need; healing, anointing, prosperity, endurance, patience, love, joy, peace, protection, good relationships, guidance, self fulfilment, anything you seek after, God has already made available to you through Grace. God won't anoint you more because you fasted or prayed. He won't heal you now because you prayed. He won't curse you, be angry at you or take away His blessings because you sinned or fell short of His standards. However, you need to exercise faith to appropriate everything God has given you by Grace. So, now what? You may say, "All I need is to be saved so I don't care for anything else, at least I'll still make it to heaven". Well, here's what the bible has to say regarding this;

You No Longer Have a Nature of Sin

Colossians 3:9-10 says *"Do not lie to one another, since you have put off the old man with his deeds, and have put on the* new *man who is renewed in knowledge according to the image of Him who created him,"*

Romans 6:6 says *"Knowing this, that our old man was crucified with Him, that the body of sin might be done away with, that we should no longer be slaves of sin"*

Through the Grace of God, your Old Nature was replaced with the nature of Christ (New Nature) which is created in Christ's righteousness. 2 Peter 1:4 says you now partake of the divine nature and you have escaped the corruption that is in the world through lust. Grace sets you free from the slavery of sin and sin consciousness[46] to righteousness consciousness so that you should not dwell in sin[47]. Paul says in Galatians 2:17-18: *"But if, while we seek to be justified by Christ, we ourselves also are found sinners, is Christ therefore a minister of sin? Certainly not!"*

At the new birth experience, you put on the New Man and you no longer have a nature of sin. Paul says in 2 Corinthians 5:17, 21 that you are now a new creature and that you are the righteousness of God in Christ. Isaiah 61:3 says we are trees of righteousness. Jesus said in Matthew 7:16-17 that every tree produces after its kind. A good tree

---

[46] *Hebrews 10:2*
[47] *1 John 3:9*

cannot bear bad fruit; likewise a bad tree cannot bear good fruit. You have received the New Nature which is of righteousness[48]; how then can you live in sin? As a believer in Christ, you are now a partaker of the divine nature of God and your spirit is holy and perfect that is why 1John 4:17 says as God is, so are you in this world. Hebrews 9:12 says Jesus has entered the Most Holy Place once for all and has obtained eternal redemption. Your sins have been paid for, God isn't angry at you anymore and the sinful nature in you has been crucified so, why would you go against your born again nature to live in sin? A born again who dwells in sin is like running uphill because the sinful nature has already been dealt with through Christ. When you perceive this truth, living a holy life won't be a work of the law. It will be a work of righteousness, a good work. The work of the Law says "live holy so God can bless you or so God won't be mad at you" but if you are born again, you no longer have a sinful nature so you live holy because God has already made you holy, because that is who you are. Holiness now becomes a byproduct, an overflow of who you are. Since we live in a fallen world, you may slip off and commit a sin, but then don't dwell in it. If you've been made the righteousness of God, how then can you dwell in sin? If you do, you never received the Grace of God by faith. Grace works by faith, and faith without works (of righteousness) is dead[49]. The Grace of God teaches you to deny ungodliness and live righteously[50] not so that God can accept you but because God has

---

[48] *Galatians 3:27*
[49] *James 2:14-26*
[50] *Titus 2:11-12*

already made you righteous; that's who you are.

God is spirit and He now relates with us through our spirit which has already been perfected in Christ. On the contrary, an unbeliever's spirit has not been perfected so, no matter what they do, they cannot be justified. However, it is your responsibility as a believer to pull out the fullness of God from your spirit and make it tangible in your soul and body. Philippians 2:12 says "work out your salvation with fear and trembling". This is referring to the salvation of the soul. So, when you become born again, God gives you a New Man that is eternally righteous. However, you have the responsibility of bringing out this righteousness from your Spirit to your soul and body by renewing not just the mind but the entire mindset[51] (underlying conscious and sub conscious philosophy which directs and controls a person's way of perception) by constant fellowship with God and meditating upon the word of God[52]. Consequently, since you are pure in your spirit, you purify yourself (in your soul). Verse 13 says *"for it is God who works in you both to will and to do for His good pleasure."* Even while you work out your salvation in your soul with fear and trembling, it's still not you, not your deeds or efforts but God who works in you if you let Him. Since your Old Man has been crucified and you no longer have a nature of sin, how then can you live in sin[53]? Ephesians 4:24 says *"...put on the new self, created to be like God in true righteousness and holiness"* –NIV. When you fall, rise up immediately and grow from strength to strength.

---

[51] *Romans 12:2, Ephesians 4:23-24*
[52] *Acts 20:32, Psalms 119:19*
[53] *Galatians 2:17, Romans 6:1-7*

Some people find it hard to fellowship boldly in God's presence because of sin. The devil condemns them through an evil conscience and makes them feel unworthy. Like Adam did, they run away from God instead of running towards Him but it shouldn't be so. You should instead run towards God when you sin or fall short. Don't let the devil steal your fellowship with God. There's now no condemnation for those in Christ Jesus. Only one person condemns – the devil through the law, for he is the accuser of the brethren[54]. Jesus has set you free from the Law of the Conscience and has given you the Law of Life in Christ Jesus. Amen! Jesus says in John 16:8-11 that the Holy Spirit convicts the world of sin, but He convicts a believer of righteousness. He witnesses that they are the righteousness of God in Christ. Satan seeks to deprive you of your fellowship with the Holy Spirit so, he'll condemn you when you fall. But it's God's desire for you to fellowship with Him. He will not cast you away from his presence[55]. While we were yet sinners, God loved us and died for us. How much more now that we've been saved and engrafted into His family, will He love us? Why not boldly (not with guilt) come to the throne of grace and obtain mercy in time of need[56]? Since it is both an abomination and hypocrisy for a good tree to bear bad fruits, live holy because you now have a New Nature.

Slave or Free?

Secondly when a person sins, s/he opens a door for the devil to

---

[54] *Revelations 12:9-10*
[55] *John 6:37*
[56] *Hebrews 4:16*

come in and torment him/her. That is exactly what Adam did and the devil took advantage of it. Romans 6:11-23 says "...*For sin shall not have dominion over you, for you are not under law but under grace.*"

Apostle Paul continues to say that you are slaves to whom you summit yourselves to obey. When you sin, you summit yourself to Satan. It may be a gradual process but one thing is certain, Satan will enslave you to obey him and you will end up saying "God is mad at me and is punishing me..." No, God does not punish His children neither is He angry at them. You have simply given room to the devil and he is eating your cake and you are letting him have it. This is one reason why many Christians are in all kinds of bondage. You have been called to liberty of the Spirit in righteousness, not Bondage. Galatians 5:13 says "*For you, brethren, have been called to liberty; only do not use liberty as an opportunity for the flesh, but through love serve one another.*" You are free to righteousness, free to live in the Spirit, free to fellowship with God. God calls you friend[57], He calls you family[58]. Don't use that liberty to be enslaved to Sin. In the Old Covenant, God was angry at the Children of Israel and He destroyed them because they had to earn His favor but His standards are insurmountably high so no one ever could. In the New Covenant, God still hates Sin but He won't be mad at His children because Jesus our Surety has redeemed us. He has wiped out the handwriting of requirements that was against us[59].

Furthermore, in the Old Covenant God dealt with the children of

---

[57] *John 15:15*
[58] *Hebrews 2:11*
[59] *Colossians 2:14*

Israel on a physical level so they had to be perfect in order to earn God's blessings. In the New Covenant however, God deals with us on a spiritual level. In our Spirits, we are Holy like Christ. We are the righteousness of God and we've been sealed with the Holy Spirit[60] so when God looks at us, He sees Christ's righteousness. 2Corinthians 2:15 says;

"For we are to God the fragrance of Christ among those who are being saved and among those who are perishing."

When God looks at you He smells Christ, He sees Christ. God is eternally happy with you and He doesn't hold your sins against you[61]. However, when you dwell in sin the devil will use that as an opportunity to deprive you of the blessings of God the same way he deprived Adam of his God-given authority. So, it is wise to abstain from sin and renew your mind to God through fellowship with His Spirit and His word, not as a work of the law but as a good work of faith.

Law of the Spirit of Life

Thirdly, if you dwell in sin, you'd lose sight of the Law of the Spirit of Life in Christ Jesus and the law of the conscience would now become alive in you. The devil will use this as an opportunity to condemn you and activate guilt in you. Hebrews 10:2 says when we are purified, we have no more consciousness of sins. When you sin, the

---

[60] *Ephesians 1:13*
[61] *Romans 4:8*

consciousness of sin revives and you end up being condemned by the devil. 1Timothy 1:19 says without faith and a good conscience, you'll shipwreck your faith. Satan through sin will suck away your faith and he'll steal away your good conscience. Isaiah 26:3 says you will be in perfect peace if your mind is stayed on God. You become what you meditate on. If you don't become it, you'll be greatly influenced by it because *"as a man thinks, so is he[62]."*

Also, Sin will open a door for the devil to torment you and deprive you of experiencing God's blessings and promises. So, although God isn't angry at you, although God's grace still shields you from His wrath, through sin you'd be at the mercy of the devil and I doubt the devil has any mercy. When you understand this, you won't live in sin. Rather, you will focus your mind on the finished works of Christ on the cross, His resurrection and the righteousness of God in you. Fellowship with God and meditate on His word. Amen!

Hardened heart

Fourthly, giving yourself to sin can lead, usually through a gradual process, to a state of hardness of heart, backsliding or apostasy. Individual acts of sin won't drive God away from you rather, they'll drive you away from God. They don't stop God's blessing in your life, rather they empower the devil to limit your ability to access and receive the blessings of God. So, when you give yourself to sin, your heart gradually becomes blinded and hardened to the spirit of God. Romans

---

[62] *Proverbs 23:7*

1:18-32 talks about people who knew God but persisted in sin to the point where their hearts became hardened[63] and non-receptive of the things of God.

As a born again, the Holy Spirit bears witness with your conscience that you are righteous[64]. If you continue to sin, you'd silence this renewed conscience[65] that bore witness of God's righteousness in you. As a result, you could grow in unbelief and hardness of heart. You will soon loss interest in the things of God. Spiritual things that used to excite you before will stop being of any interest to you. You may still go to church, or pray or participate in religious activities but you'll be like an empty shell. This may not be instantaneous; It may be a gradual process and could lead to a state of apostasy. That's why Apostle Paul says in 2Corinthians 13:5; *"Examine yourselves as to whether you are in the faith. Test yourselves. Do you not know yourselves that Jesus Christ is in you?* A heart that is hardened towards God cannot receive anything from God. The gifts of God are spiritually discerned and a carnal man cannot receive anything from God. When you live in sin or if you do not fellowship with God, your heart will become "dull" and "insensitive" towards the spirit of God. God will continue to speak to you, He's already blessed you, He'll reach out to you but your hardened heart would have lost its receptibility towards Him. It'll be like trying to conduct electricity through a piece of wood.

---

[63] *Isaiah 6:9-11, Acts 28:27*
[64] *Romans 9:1*
[65] *1 Timothy 4:2*

The Love of God Constrains

The most important reason to me why I fellowship with God, why I pray, why I fast, why I worship God, why I do things that please God and my motivation for living godly is the love of God. When you understand how much God loves you and how much He's done for you, sin will not have power over you. Fellowship with God, praying and studying the bible will not be an activity or obligation. It will be sweet and enjoyable. I love reading my bible not because I'm looking for my next message or researching the contents of my next book. I don't enjoy preaching as much as I do reading my bible. I love praying, I love worshipping God because I just love God. When I identify a weakness in my life, I automatically repent of it and receive grace to overcome it just because I love God. I love what He loves and hate what He hates. The love of God has been poured out in your heart by the Holy Spirit[66] and this love would compel you[67] not to sin because Love does not rejoice in sin[68]. When you love someone, you want to make them happy. You won't keep doing things you know they dislike. Rather, you do things that will please them not because you want them to accept you but because you enjoy seeing them happy. You know God delights in holiness and hates sin, so although God won't punish you for your weaknesses, you still cease from living a sinful life because you love Him. When you understand the Love of God, your motivation for living righteously would not be fear of hell or

---

[66] *Romans 5:5*
[67] *2Corinthians 5:14*
[68] *Romans 13*

condemnation or God's wrath; rather, you would live righteously because that is who you are, because you love God. You would pray and have fellowship with God because you love Him not because you are trying to "bribe" Him to bless you. Praying and studying the word of God will cease to be an activity. It will become a way of life, a product of Love. I don't have fellowship with my family because I want them to love me, I do because I already love my family and because they already love me too. Even when you live righteously, if you are motivated by anything other than the love of God, you have done nothing[69]. That good work, though it may benefit the one to whom it was done, it is counted as unprofitable to the one who did it if it wasn't motivated by the Love of God. So having this mindset, the things that you do won't be the works of the law that seeks to be justified rather, your deeds would be works of faith; they would be good works.

There's a big difference between works of the Law and works of faith or good works. Trying to earn God's blessings by the things you do are works of the law; they are dead works but doing the same things because you have faith in what Jesus has already done, motivated by the love of God is good works. I pray because I love God, I abstain from sin because I love God, when I'm in need, I go to God for help because I love God. I do none of these because I want God to see my efforts and bless me. One person can pray to God thinking that God will be impressed and answer while another person may pray for the

---

[69] *1 Corinthians 13:1-3*

same thing because s/he loves God which activates his/her faith and trust in God. Both people will have totally different results. The good news is God has empowered you to live holy. Through the word of God and the Holy Spirit, you will receive God's strength to live Holy. It won't be by your strength but by the Grace of God through faith. Apostle Paul said in Galatians 2:20; *"I have been crucified with Christ; it is no longer I who live, but Christ lives in me; and the life which I now live in the flesh I live by faith in the Son of God, who loved me and gave Himself for me."*

When you are weak, Christ will empower you. Amen! 1John 4:16 says *"…he who abides in love abides in God"*.

Ephesians 1:4 says *"we should be holy and without blame before Him (God) in love."*

Ephesians 3:17-19 says that if you are rooted in love and if you get to experience the love of God, you will be filled with the fullness of God. It's all about the love of God. Therefore, let the love of God be your motivation in everything you do or think. Don't let sin have dominion over you, because you are not under law but under grace[70]. Amen!

---

[70] *Romans 6:11-23*

CHAPTER FOUR
NEWNESS OF LIFE IN CHRIST JESUS

Unconditional Love

God created us, all of us and like a mother to her child, He loves us tremendously. We can't fathom the extent of His love for us. Because we were born in a fallen world, our natural concept of love has been thwarted so many people tend to approach God based on their un-pure notion of love and relationship. Philippians 2:13 says;

"for it is God who works in you both to will and to do for His good pleasure".

Ephesians 1:5 says;

"...having predestined us to adoption as sons by Jesus Christ to Himself, according to the good pleasure of His will..."

The Greek word for "pleasure" in these scriptures is *"eudokia"* and it means good will, kind intention, benevolence. God created us out of and for Love, not for servitude. He already has myriads upon myriads of innumerable Angels[1] who serve Him and His children[2] so God doesn't need us to be His errand men and women. He can perfectly fulfill His every will without human beings if that was more important to Him than His word. I have a daughter whom I love so much. My wife and I didn't conceive her because we wanted somebody to assist with house chores. If that was our primary concern, we would have

---

[1] *Revelations 5:11, Daniel 7:10, Hebrews 12:22,*
[2] *Hebrews 1:7, 14*

hired the services of a maid. We weren't thinking about having somebody to take care of us at our old age. Children can and should do these things for their parents but that's not the reason she was conceived. We had her for our good pleasure. Just having a child who came from us, who shared our DNA and looked like us just makes us feel happy and proud. Every time I look at our daughter and see how she lives freely and smiles and just walks around the house without taking deep thoughts of anything makes us feel blessed. It's even more so with God. He created us for the pleasure of His will, because He loves us. God wants to have a warm fellowship with you, because He loves you unconditionally. Jesus said in John 15:15;

"No longer do I call you servants, for a servant does not know what his master is doing; but I have called you friends, for all things that I heard from My Father I have made known to you."

Shortly after His resurrection, Jesus said in John 20:17b;

"...but go to My brethren and say to them, 'I am ascending to My Father and your Father, and to My God and your God.'"

Hebrews 2:11 says;

"For both He who sanctifies and those who are being sanctified are all of one, for which reason He is not ashamed to call them brethren,"

God, creator of the universe, all powerful, full of glory and splendor loves us so much that He made us one with Him and He's not ashamed to call us friends and brethren. Our society is stratified into different types of classes. The rich deride the poor, people from different races and ethnic groups are prejudiced against each other, even in churches we see contempt and prejudices across different religious class constructs. But God who is the greatest and ranks infinitely superior to any class loves mere mortals like us and calls us friends, family. If He went to the extent of sacrificing His life just to draw us closer to Himself, we can be confident and assured that His love and blessings towards us is not conditioned on what we do.

I lived in a relatively big house while growing up. We had a big yard with lots of fruit trees and flower plants so there was always a need to clean up the leaves that fell from these plants. So, my parents taught me how to do house chores, not because they wanted to make of me their servant but because they wanted me to grow up and be a responsible young man. When I was grown, they didn't have to ask me to clean my room or sweep the leaves or do any of these things; I knew my parents loved me and because they'd brought me up right, I wanted to reciprocate their love. I wanted to honor them so I would, on my own volition do these house chores. My parents took care of me whether or not I did my chores. Now that I'm grown I choose to do these chores because I love my parents and want to show my appreciation and sense of identity as a member of our family. This is the same way God wants us to relate with Him. The people of the Old Covenant were spiritually immature so like a child, they had to learn how to please God. Serving God was like a chore, it was an obligation. But now, through the death and resurrection of Jesus our spirits are now alive to God and we're synced with God. We are no longer slaves or servants; Jesus said God is now our friend, our father. We are God's family. He wants us to fellowship with Him out of love, and not out of obligation. That is what Apostle Paul meant by the love Christ compels us – 2Corinthians 5:14. God created us for His pleasure to be not just creations but sons[3], joint heirs with Christ[4]. He has already blessed us[5] and He already loves us even when we didn't qualify, even when we were sinners[6].

God Chose to Love

Our fallen world has thwarted the true meaning of love. God's kind of love is not based on a feeling or an emotion, it's a conscious decision, and it's a choice. God chose to love you not because you are lovely but because He is love. If I loved my spouse because I was emotionally attracted to her looks, personality, the way she made me feel, etc. what would happen if she lost those looks or good behavior, personality, etc.? In essence, I would be in love with her looks, personality, good behavior, socio-economic status, etc. but not her person. So, if I met someone else who had or exceeded my spouse's qualities or who was able to stir up my emotions better than my wife, what would stop me from chasing after another woman? If I merely endured our relationship because I didn't want to hurt her feelings although I lust after someone else who surpassed her, would I say I loved her? 2Corinthians 5:16 says *"Therefore, from now on, we regard no one*

---

[3] *Galatians 3:26, John 1:12*
[4] *Romans 8:17*
[5] *Ephesians 1:3, 2 Peter 1:3*
[6] *Romans 5:8*

according to the flesh." Any type of relationship that is built on the foundations of emotions is built on shaky grounds. Emotions are a response to the things we experience; emotions come and go. You can't feel happy for ever, sometimes you'd feel sad, then happy, then anxious, then angry, then love, then hate. Sometimes you'll feel anger or hate even towards the person you love the most. Your mood and emotions would fluctuate depending on the things that happen around you.

Our society defines love as a feeling; an emotional response or an intense feeling of deep affection but the truth is God doesn't love you emotionally. He chose to love you that is why although we were sinners, our sins didn't stop Him from loving us. If God's love was conditioned by our acts of goodness or obedience to His word, it wouldn't be Love by God's standards. If God loved us in proportion of how much we made Him feel emotionally happy, no human being would still be alive; He would have long wiped out the whole world. Thank God that His love for us is unconditional[7]. It's amazing, and reassuring to know that God chose to love me and His love for me isn't fragile. He first loved us so we can love Him in return. Would you still stay true to God if you didn't seem to receive the answers to your prayers or if you didn't see His goodness in your life? What about that preacher whom you once loved with God's kind of love but who fell through the cracks or sinned or said something you didn't agree with? Do you join the crowd in telling the world how the man of God has

---

[7] *Ephesians 2:8*

fallen thereby exposing God's family, your family of God to the world? If God loved us and emotionally responded to us based on the things we did, I guarantee the world would have long ceased to exist.

God chose to love you and wants you to express your sincere love for Him first and above any acts of righteousness. Even if the devil didn't exist and even if he didn't come after me, I would still fellowship with God because I love Him; not because I want Him to bless me although He has blessed me non-the-less. This is amazing!

God is a Good God

I used to ask myself why there's so much evil around us today; floods, disasters, starvation, injustice, hatred, etc. then I realized, indeed God is a good God. The bible says God is good, and what He does is good[8]. God's goodness and love lasts forever[9]. *The Lord is good to all; He has compassion on all He has made*[10]. Every good and every perfect gift comes from God[11]. On the contrary, the devil is a liar and a deceiver[12] and he comes to steal, kill and destroy[13]. All the evil in this world is caused by Satan but why would God allow it? The truth is, God doesn't allow it; we, believers allow it. God has already restored us to a place of authority over this earth and over the devil, and He has restored our right and ability to choose for ourselves but we have allowed all the evil to occur. Ephesians 3:10 says *"to the intent that now*

---

[8] *Psalms 119:68; Psalms 86:5; Psalms 100:5; Psalms 106:1; Psalms 107:1*
[9] *Psalms 107:1*
[10] *Psalms 145:9*
[11] *James 1:17*
[12] *John 8:44, 2Corinthians 11:3, Revelation 12:9*
[13] *1Peter 5:8, Ephesians 6:16, John 10:10*

the manifold wisdom of God might be made known **by the church to the principalities and powers** *in the heavenly places*". Jesus said in Luke 10:19 that He had given us authority to trample over snakes and scorpions and all the power of the enemy. Jesus' last words before ascending to heaven in Mark 16 was to go into all the world and preach the gospel... casting out demons, healing the sick. It's our responsibility as children of God and co-heirs with Christ to stop the works of the devil on earth. Our role just like Adam's is to "tend the garden", tend to our world. If the garden of Eden was well kept, it wouldn't be God's fault because He'd already tasked Adam to tend it. The responsibility of making this world a better place is not on God or the government, it's on the Church, it's on every born again believer. God is eternally good and just so if you are born again, know that you've been born of a good God who truly loves and cares about you. He literally died for you. The bible says we are inscribed on the palms of His hands[14]; He sees your name every day and looks for ways to show His love to you. God is not the cause of your suffering or sorrow or anything evil, neither is He the cause of the evil in the world. God doesn't kill babies; He doesn't kill our siblings, relatives or loved ones. He doesn't need them in heaven more than we do on earth either. God already has countless Angels to minister before Him, He needs your loved ones more on earth to tend to the world and preach the gospel of peace. If I killed your loved ones and told you I needed them more in the land of the dead, would you say I am loving? If I caused sickness,

---

[14] *Isaiah 49:16*

poverty, bad relationships, earthquakes and tremors, hatred, injustice and all sought of disasters, would you call me a good person? The courts would send me to prison. God certainly isn't the cause of evil and He doesn't allow it either, but He has restored our authority over the devil so we now have a choice of whether or not to exercise that authority. Be assured that God is good and He wants to give you every good thing. Amen!

Welcome Home!

"But you have come to Mount Zion and to the city of the living God, the heavenly Jerusalem, to an innumerable company of angels, to the general assembly and church of the firstborn who are registered in heaven, to God the Judge of all, to the spirits of just men made perfect, to Jesus the Mediator of the new covenant, and to the blood of sprinkling that speaks better things than that of Abel." – Hebrews 12:22-24

This is God's welcome message to anyone who has or wants to become His child. When you give your life to Christ and become born again, you don't merely join a church and start doing religious activities. No! You've been called to a place of fellowship with God. You've been called to a realm that surpasses this earthly realm. It's like going to your new job on the first day and at the onboarding meeting, the CEO comes up and says *"You have come to Mount Zion, the city of the Living God…to an innumerable company of angels…and to the blood of sprinkling that speaks better things than that of Abel."* Angels are ministering Spirits[15] who have been sent by God to serve you. God, in His onboarding message

---

[15] *Hebrews 1:14*

says you've come to an innumerable company of ministering Spirits sent to serve you, why? - Because God loves you immensely that He assigned powerful angels to take care of you. Just imagine how you'd feel if the president of your country sent his most skillful secret agents to serve and protect you. Angels are infinitely stronger and superior to human beings, but God chose to assign them to us, to serve us. That's how much He loves us. He has made you a joint heir with Him which means you now have access to everything God possesses. Isaiah 54:10 says;

"For the mountains shall depart and the hills be removed, But My kindness shall not depart from you, nor shall My covenant of peace be removed," Says the Lord, who has mercy on you."

The CEV versions puts it this way; *"...But I will always be kind and merciful to you."* Let me repeat this so it resonates in your heart. God says "I WILL ALWAYS BE KIND TO YOU. Apostle Paul says NOTHING can separate us from the love of Christ[16].

In your onboarding message, God says your Spirit is now alive to His Spirit and unlike the Old Covenant prophets, you can now spiritually discern the things of God. You don't need an Angel to physically bring the answers to your prayers the way He did in the Old Covenant. God now dwells within you. 2Corinthians 13:5 says *"...Do you not know yourselves, that Jesus Christ is in you?"* 2Corinthians 4:6-7 says *"For it is the God who commanded light to shine out of darkness, who has shone*

---

[16] *Romans 8:38-39*

in our hearts to give the light of the knowledge of the glory of God in the face of Jesus Christ. Cast Down but Unconquered But we have this treasure in earthen vessels that the excellence of the power may be of God and not of us."

The bible is full of promises like this. God in you is a treasure. The people of the Old Covenant didn't have this treasure. Some of their prophets had a glimpse of it, they saw it from afar but couldn't touch it. The Spirit of God always came upon them but never dwelt in them. Their spirits were blind to (separated from) God so God couldn't dwell in them. But we have God living in us. Isn't this an amazing onboarding message? Unlike Daniel who needed the answers to his prayers to be delivered to him physically, you now have God living inside of you from whence He answers your prayers and flows to the rest of the world. John 7:38-39 says;

"He who believes in Me, as the Scripture has said, out of his heart will flow rivers of living water." But this He spoke concerning the Spirit, whom those believing in Him would receive; **for the Holy Spirit was not yet given, because Jesus was not yet glorified"**

The devil can no longer directly or physically hinder your prayers. What he can do however is tempt you to doubt or entice you with weights, distractions, unbelieve or sins to the point where your heart becomes hardened or insensitive to God. He can redirect your attention away from God towards anything that will destroy your faith but he can't physically or directly interfere with your prayers anymore like he did in the days of Daniel. If you let him succeed, you'd have hindered your prayers yourself. It's for this reason that 2Corinthians 2:11 says *"lest*

Satan should take advantage of us; for we are not ignorant of his devices."

In the Old Covenant, people cast lots or sought for some physical sign to confirm the will of God but now, you have the Holy Spirit living right inside you. You no longer need to wait for physical signs to determine the will of God. In Acts 1:26, the disciples cast lots to determine who God chose to replace Judas Iscariot because the Holy Spirit had not yet come. After they received the Holy Spirit they no longer needed a physical sign, the Holy Spirit spoke to them and gave them directions. The Holy Spirit lives inside you and He's your personal Knowledge Management System. He will tell you the mind and intent of God, He will direct you and He will teach you to hear His voice. He will guide you towards all truth as you begin to enjoy the greater blessings of God. This is an awesome onboarding, welcome message, Amen!

CHAPTER FIVE
WALKING IN A FRESH MIND

Newness of Mind

The word of God promises us so many blessings but sometimes we don't seem to physically and tangibly see them in our lives. Consequently, we tend to be discouraged and we lose faith in the word of God. Some people then tend to pursue their own avenues of getting what they seek. I was talking with a friend some time ago and she said blatantly that God didn't love her. She couldn't understand why she wasn't able to experience any positive results from God. This kind of attitude is likely to emerge when we don't experience the promises of God in a physically tangible way; We'd tend to either disbelieve when people testify of God's blessings, or we'd disbelieve the word of God altogether but know that God has exalted us and we now have access to the fullness of God. We have the higher life in Christ and we partake as heirs of the full resources of God through Christ so we need to act upon the word of God with faith and patience.

The kingdom of God suffers violence and the violent shall take it by force. This phrase doesn't mean using physical force, rather it means to be actively involved in the things of God with eager self-interest. Apostle Peter said *"Be careful! Watch out for attacks from the Devil, your great enemy. He prowls around like a roaring lion, looking for some victim to devour"*- 1Peter 5:8, NLT. This means he cannot devour everybody or anybody. If that were the case, he wouldn't be looking for someone, he'd just devour anyone. Don't be his victim! We've seen in the earlier chapters that the principal way through which the devil can eat your cake and have it is if you rent him space in your mind. The battle is in the mind. In 2Corinthians 10:3-5, Apostle Paul talking about spiritual warfare says;

"For though we walk in the flesh, we do not war according to the flesh. For the weapons of our warfare are not carnal but mighty in God for pulling down strongholds, **casting down arguments and every high thing that exalts itself against the knowledge of God, bringing every thought into captivity to the obedience of Christ."**

Romans 12:2 says *"Don't copy the behavior and customs of this world, but be a new and different person with a fresh newness in all you do and think. Then you will learn from your own experience how his ways will really satisfy you"* –TLB. Paul is saying that the battle is in the mind; the way you can experience the ways of God that will satisfy you is by renewing your mind to conform to God's word, and the way you do that is to live daily for God and letting His Word dwell in you richly. Amen! Your mind was given to you by God to exercise yourself unto godliness and not to worry yourself about the things of this world. Am I saying you should neglect your body and physical needs? No! I am saying you shouldn't let them deprive you of the fullness of God, because Satan will pass through your worries to get to you. Isaiah 26:3 says *"You will keep him in perfect peace, whose mind is stayed on You, because he trusts in You"*

One major reason a lot of Christians don't see the blessings of God manifest in their lives as they should is, they rely more on their carnal senses – what they see, feel, taste, smell, hear and touch. God's promises are to be accepted by faith which means it may not make sense to the physical senses. Our Spirits are alive to God so He no longer needs to physically come to us like He did in the Old Covenant. The bible says what is seen is temporary but what is not seen is eternal so, the troubles you encounter, though they seem real to your carnal senses, they are not your reality. They are temporary and virtual…unless you accept them as your reality through your mind. Everything that the word of God does not say is unreal but every promise of God through His word defines your reality irrespective of what you physically experience or feel.

I saw a movie some time ago where the protagonist used a technological device called a hologram to create a virtual 3D image of himself. This image was so real that the enemy thought it was a real person but it was merely a holographic image. The protagonist used this virtual image to deceive the bad guys which gave him the advantage. That's what the devil does when he brings all the negative things you see, feel, hear, smell, taste, and experience. He wants to deceive you through these unreal things, so you'll be distracted from receiving the greater blessings of God. Sometimes however, the devil may have nothing to do with the things you experience. We live in a fallen world and even without the active efforts of the devil, some negative things might still happen to us. But, you are a heavenly being and your reality is from heaven; your reality is defined by everything God says. If you understand that you are a spirit being that has a soul and lives in a body[1], whenever the things of the soul or of the body come up, you'll immediately recognize that they are not your reality. Your reality is in the Spirit, sustained by the word of God. You may ask; "this sickness I am suffering from, are you saying it is not real? What about all these tangible pains and symptoms? I can't pay my bills, I'm going through a divorce, I have cancer and I will soon die, are you saying I am dreaming?" Well that's the problem. You believe it's real because your carnal senses say so. Physically, you experience the pains of sickness, bills to pay, relationship issues, depression, anxiety, fear, etc. but those physical things don't define your reality. You are a spirit being living in a physical body. Your physical body is merely a vessel that houses the real you which is spirit. Your source is not from the earth but from the Spirit of God. It's like a person dying of hunger when they have millions in their bank account. Their reality is what's in the bank account so, as long as they stay connected to their bank, they'll be able to purchase an entire restaurant if they have to. When you are sick the reality is, by His stripes you were healed[2]. The reality is, God has given you power to heal the sick[3]. The reality is, God sent His word and healed your diseases[4]. When you are broke the reality is, it's God who teaches you to make wealth[5]. The reality is, God has blessed you with everything that pertains to life and godliness[6]. The

---

[1] *1 Thessalonians 5:23*
[2] *Isaiah 53:5; 1 Peter 2:24*
[3] *Mark 16:15-18*
[4] *Psalm 107:20*
[5] *Deuteronomy 8:17-18*
[6] *2 Peter 1:3*

reality is, don't worry about tomorrow, seek ye first the kingdom of God and all His righteousness and all other things shall be added unto you[7]. The reality is, give and it shall be given unto you, pressed down, shaken together and running over[8]. For every crises you face in life, God has defined your reality in His word.

In 2 kings 6, the Arameans who were enemies of Israel sought to capture prophet Elisha because he was foiling their battle plans to defeat Israel. So, the King of Aram sent his armies to capture prophet Elisha at Dothan[9]. As their armies circled around the city, Gehazi, Elisha's servant began to get worried. He was relying on what his eyes and feelings were tell him. Everyone including Elisha could physically see the armies of the enemy but Elisha knew his physical experience did not define his reality. Elisha prayed and God opened the eyes of Gehazi and behold, Gehazi saw the mountains full of heavenly horses and chariots of fire all around Elisha. Then Elisha prayed and all his enemies were struck with blindness. Elisha didn't rely on what he saw or felt, he knew his reality was in God. The chariots of God were always around Elisha, they didn't only appear when he was in trouble, they were always there. If Elisha relied on his physical senses, he would have been defeated by the enemy. Do you now understand how important it is to rely on the word of God and make it your reality? The crises you encounter work like a spell. If you are under a spell, you

---

[7] Matthew 6:33-34
[8] Luke 6:38
[9] Ancient City of Dothan was located north of Shechem, about 12 miles to the north of Samaria.

may be walking towards a flower garden but the spell may make you see a ravine instead and it'll appear so real to you. But once you know the reality, the spell won't be as effective anymore.

Whenever you are in a physical dilemma, the solution is already right there but it's in the spirit so you can't access it through your physical senses. The word of God that defines your reality says by His stripes, you were healed. Meaning, if it is true that Jesus died and rose again; then it is also true that He took away your sickness and infirmity because healing is part of the salvation package. If He said you should not worry about tomorrow; what you'll wear and eat but you should focus your mind on Him and He'll meet the needs of your body, then that's your reality. If His word says that He has blessed you with everything that pertains to life and godliness and that He has wiped away the handwriting of requirements that was against you, then anything that is contrary to this is a distraction, a "spell", a ruse to hinder you from receiving from God. Although your natural senses feel differently, although you may physically experience or go through the crisis, when you understand that the just shall live by faith, and you know that God's word is your source that defines your reality, who you really are, you won't be moved. So, train your mind to conform to God's word because the mind is the gateway that releases the power of God from the spirit realm to this earthly dimension. 2Corinthians 5:7 says we walk by faith (trusting in what God has said) not by sight (what our human senses reveal to us). Proverbs 3:5 says *"Trust in the LORD with all your heart, and lean not on your own understanding"* (what your human senses say to you). So when you have a crisis, go to the Word of God and cling to it like glue till your natural senses do the same. The devil and the cares of this world will not take a back seat and let you go after the things of God. So, you'll have to be violent, go after the word and promises of God with eager self-interest. Make God your priority. God gives us His word and it's our responsibility to build on that word till it begins to work in our lives. In one of His last exhortations to His disciples Jesus said, *"in the world you shall have tribulation but be of good cheer, I have overcome the world"*-John 16:33. What Jesus is saying here is, I (God) have given you victory and that defines your reality so when tribulations come your way, don't worry and don't lose your peace. This is indeed a mystery that a carnal mind cannot understand[10] but as a child of God, you have obtained the Spirit of God by which you can understand the mysteries of God[11].

You may ask yourself: "from what then should I renew my mind?"- From all the junk we see and hear on a daily basis; all sorts of negative news, information from the internet, people crying and complaining here and there, unemployment, world crisis, and all such things pollute your mind and you become unconsciously and negatively influenced by them. You gradually begin to accept and ponder upon them. These things suck out your faith and before you know it, you're down. When you see all the evil around you, you'll be tempted to speak like the carnal man; "If God loves the world, why is

---

[10] *1 Corinthians 1:18; 2:14*
[11] *Ephesians 1:9; Colossians 1:26; 1 Corinthians 2:9-10*

there so much sorrow, hunger, negativity, evil, injustice, suffering, etc. all around the world?" Well, the bible says the earth is full of the goodness of God[12]. Yes, there's evil in the world but we and our local news media amplify them out of proportion; When we read the Old Testament, we see that the evil back then was much greater than the evil we see today but advancement in media technology today makes it possible to receive news from all over the world within seconds so it feels like the world will burn within the next hour. Turn on your gospel channels and you'll see millions of people all around the world serving and loving God and just receiving miracles every day. The news will report about people who died of cancer but will not report about those who received God's healing all over the world. The news will report on armed robbery and murder, racism, world hunger and all sorts of negative things but will not report on the positive things that God is doing in our neighborhoods every single day through His children and our local churches. God is good and I know there's more goodness in the world than we realize. We live in a fallen world and Satan still rules the hearts of many people so, there's bound to be some evil. Non-the-less, God's goodness still prevails in this world because the Holy Spirit is still here and God's family is still on earth. Yes, the bible says in the last days iniquity shall abound, it also says in the latter days God shall poor out His Spirit upon all flesh[13]. Would you focus on the evil or on the Spirit of God? Choose to ponder upon those things that have

---

[12] *Psalms 33:5*
[13] *Matt 24:12; Joel 2:28; Acts 2:17*

virtue and are of good report[14]. Make the Word of God your reality!

What You Know and Meditate On

You are influenced by what you meditate on – whether fear leading to depression and defeat or faith leading to a victorious life in Christ.

There is a prophet in the bible whom I believe is one of the greatest prophets in the Old Testament; his name is Elijah. Even Elisha who did twice as much as Elijah and John the Baptist who was the greatest man born of a woman under the Old Covenant both had the spirit of Elijah. Prophet Elijah was the first person in scripture to raise the dead, he commanded fire from heaven to consumed his sacrifice, he killed 450 false prophets in one day[15], he outran the chariot of King Ahab on foot, he held the rain and commanded the rain to fall, and the list goes on. This is a man whom God supernaturally fed through a raven. When Queen Jezebel, wife of King Ahab heard that Prophet Elijah had murdered the prophets of Baal, she sent a messenger to inform him that she has taken an oath to murder him. This information built fear in Elijah. He knew very well that Jezebel had not murdered all the prophets yet he chose to allow fear cripple him. He forgot about the miracles God had done through him; he did not remember that he'd killed over 450 men in one day; he did not remember how he'd done all these countless miracles, even raising the dead. He could have commanded fire from heaven to destroy Jezebel if he wanted to. The problem was not Jezebel or what she could do to him; the problem

---

[14]*Philippians 4:8*
[15] *1Kings 18:18-40*

was what he meditated on. "Mighty" Elijah was already defeated in his mind by a mere note from a "nobody" because he pondered on the threat made to him. Instead of meditating on God who could save him, he started complaining out of fear. He said Jezebel had murdered all the prophets of God and he was the only one left but this was a lie; He was so afraid that He lied to God. He even asked God to take His life. Elijah knew very well that there were other prophets alive because Obadiah had informed him earlier about the other prophets he hid in the caves[16]. This is exactly what happens when you focus your mind on the negative things that happen around you. They systematically build fear and defeat in you. What "note" have you received from "whom" that is making you lose your peace? Is it a doctor's note that says you are sick and can't get well or is it a note from your bank account that says your bills can't be paid? Is it a note from society that says your future is uncertain? Or a note from the devil that says you are not good enough? What situation in your life is threatening your peace and joy? The problem is not the "note" you received or what it can do to you but what you meditate on.

In many cultures in Africa, Asia and Native America, the owl is seen as an evil bird that has a bad omen. So, fear would haunt an average person from any of these cultures when they see or hear an owl within their neighborhood. If somebody who didn't have this knowledge saw the same owl, s/he'd gladly take pictures of it and play with it. The same object but different response from different people

---

[16] *1 Kings 18:13*

because of the information they have received. In the same way, the negative things that happen around us; the economic crisis, sicknesses, the immorality we see and hear on T.V., and all the junk that happens around us build an information system in our minds that will produce an undesirable output. Once a negative mindset has run its course, we will end up with a less that optimum result. That is why a continual renewing of the mind is indispensable for every child of God who wants to walk in the greater blessings of God.

How to Renew Your Mind

As children of God, we are beneficiaries of God's blessings and promises but a lot of times we don't experience these blessings to the full extent that God intents. One major reason is, our minds fail to align with the word of God as it should. Ephesians 4:23 says be renewed in the spirit (attitude) of your mind. This is not merely talking about changing your thoughts; It is talking about changing the attitude of your mind; renewing your mindset and the way you think. Paul says in Ephesians 1:18 *"I ask that your minds may be opened to see his light, so that you will know what is the hope to which he has called you, how rich are the wonderful blessings he promises his people"* –TEV.

The first way of renewing your mind is by studying and meditating on the word of God. Believe what the word of God says to build faith then act upon it. The word "meditate" (*Greek: meletaō*) means to ponder or imagine (to have a mental image of God's word), i.e. to practice in your mind or to have a mental image of the word of God in your mind. So when you study the word of God, make it a habit to practice it with your mind. Through your mind, see yourself walking in and manifesting what the word of God says. Apostle Paul says in Acts 20:32 that the word of God is able to give you an inheritance among the saints. The word of God is living and powerful and it is Spirit, it is capable of discerning and changing your mind to align with what God says[17]. How much you get from the word of God depends on how much of it you've worked out in your mind. 2Corinthians 3:18 says; *"But we all, with unveiled face, beholding as in a mirror the glory of the Lord, are being transformed into the same image from glory to glory, just as by the Spirit of the Lord."*

The word of God is so essential to every born again because it is the seed or "spiritual semen" through which we were reborn at the new birth experience. 1Peter 1:23 says: *"Having been born again, not of corruptible seed but incorruptible, through the word of God which lives and abides forever".*

The message version puts it this way;

"Your new life is not like your old life. Your old birth came from mortal sperm; your new birth comes from God's living Word."

The word of God is your life! It's the seed or "sperm" that birthed you into God's family and it is the seed that will birth every blessing in your life! If you wait for perfect conditions before you start doing what the word of God says, you will never get anything done. Ecclesiastes 11:4 says; *"If you wait for perfect conditions, you will never get anything done"* –NLT.

---

[17]*Hebrews 4:12*

Don't just read the bible, meditate on it, and practice it in your mind.

In addition to meditating on the word of God, pray always in the spirit. Praying in tongues is extremely important for every believer. By praying in tongues, you engage in a language of the spirit. So, when you make it a habit of praying in tongues, you align your soul with the realities of the spirit and before you know it, you'll be experiencing what the word of God says and even your emotions will begin to express the will and ways of God. 1Corinthians 14:4 says you edify yourself when you pray in tongues. Jude 1:20 says that the way you build yourself on your most holy faith is by praying in tongues. When you pray in tongues, it is your spirit that is perfect and knows the mind of God that prays. Sooner or later, your mind will begin to conform to your spirit. Ephesians 6:18 Says *"praying always with all prayer and supplication in the Spirit…."* Apostle Paul understood how important this was so he boldly told the church in Corinth that he prayed in tongues more than all of them[18]. Imagine one man praying in tongues more than an entire congregation of believers. What a radical claim! He prayed in tongues, sang in tongues, prophesied in tongues, he did everything in tongues and you notice that Apostle Paul was one of the greatest if not, the greatest of all the Apostles in terms of the things he did and said in recorded scripture. He experienced God in his life and ministry in a tremendous way. He goes on to say in 1Corinthians 14:39 that *"do not forbid to speak with tongues."* It's not within the scope of this book to teach on tongues but I encourage you to do a study on it and

---

[18] *1Corinthians 14:18*

if you have doubts, be assured that the Holy Spirit is your ultimate teacher and He'll teach you if you're willing and sincere. If you do not speak in tongues yet (the Holy Spirit is the one that gives you utterance to speak in tongues), I encourage you to desire it, ask God for it and you'll receive it. Amen!

Finally, Ephesians 6:13-14 says *"…having done all to stand, stand therefore…."* So, start by meditating on the word of God and praying in tongues always. Watch your attitude, allow the Holy Spirit to freely give you His opinion. Obey and do what the council of God's word says even if it looks foolish or impossible and God is not unjust to forget your work and labor of love which you have shown toward His name, Amen!

Living Daily For God

I have seen many Christians attend revival meetings where they get so blessed and spiritually energized but when they return from such meetings, the zeal that was ignited in them burns only for a week or two after which they revert back to their "old selves." One reason Christians lose their zeal shortly after attending an impactful spiritual retreat is that they don't live daily for God. They think they can accumulate the anointing to last a while but they fail to realize that the anointing is sustained daily. What God really wants is that you live daily for Him. It's a daily walk with God! King David said in Psalm 139:16;

"You saw me before I was born. Every day of my life was recorded in your book. Every moment was laid out before a single day had passed" –NLT.

David is saying here that before he was created, God had planned every single day, every single moment of his life. Walking daily with God means living according to what He has planned for you on a daily basis; being conscious of Christ on a daily basis. Jesus, teaching about living daily for God says you should not worry about tomorrow for sufficient for today is its own troubles[19]. In verse 33, Jesus said *"But seek first the kingdom of God and His righteousness, and all these things shall be added to you."* Putting verses 33 and 34 together, Jesus is saying that you should seek God every day, on a daily basis and He'll meet your daily needs. Renew your mind in God every day, every moment of your life. Lamentations 3:23 – 24 says the mercies and compassion of God are renewed every morning. God renews His grace to live for him on a daily basis. King David in Psalm 118:24 says "This is the day the Lord has made; we will rejoice and be glad in it." God provided manna to Israel daily. They weren't allowed to keep extra manna for the next day except during Sabbath. In Acts 2:2-4, the Apostles were filled with the Holy Spirit for the first time, but in chapter 4:31, they were refilled with the Holy Spirit a second time and so on. When they were persecuted, their minds were inflicted with discouragement, fear and everything that comes with it. So, Apostle Peter who had been bold enough to preach to a crowd of more than 5000 people on the day of Pentecost was becoming weak in his mind as well as all the other Christians who were being persecuted. Together with other disciples, they prayed that God would give them strength over the threats of the Pharisees and

---

19*Matthew 6:33-34*

boldness to preach the gospel with power. What they heard and saw was contaminating their minds, but after praying, they were refreshed. Every day, you will be tempted and your mind will receive negativity so you need to be refreshed in your mind daily. Fellowship with God daily, as if there were no tomorrow. Study and meditate on the word of God daily, as if there were no tomorrow. Don't be a seasonal or Sunday Christian. The secret of living a steady victorious Christian life is to renew your mind and live for God daily. Amen!

CHAPTER SIX
EXPERIENCE GOD'S GREATER BLESSINGS

Everything we've talked about up to this point leads to this chapter. God loves you and He wants to bless you. The devil on the other hand doesn't want you to freely enjoy God's goodness so he'll condemn you; he'll say you are not worthy, he'll accuse you and try to keep you bound so he can steal from you. It's been a long ride up to this point so before going much further, let's do a quick review;

God created Adam and Eve and loved them freely. He gave them authority over His earthly creation and He blessed them with everything they needed; There was no sickness, no failure, no earthquakes or catastrophes, no stress or depression, no poverty, no enmity; no deaths, and carnivores ate grass and herbs[1]. God provided all of Adam and Eve's needs and they fellowshipped with Him without any strain or worry. Everything was perfect! However when Adam sinned, the devil took over Adam's authority and corrupted every blessing Adam had received. Lions that formerly ate herbs became carnivorous predators. Germs, bacteria and viruses began to cause all kind of sicknesses. Demons who were now the new rulers of this earth instead of Adam and Eve began to cause all kinds of chaos. Through Sin, Adam and Eve lost their blessing. So, God established the Old Covenant with Moses whereby the children of Israel had to earn their blessings through their own efforts but God's standards were so high

---

[1] *Genesis 1:29-30*

that no one could ever earn their blessings. This was all in preparation for the New Covenant. Now, we relate with God based on the provisions of the New Covenant whereby Christ is our High Priest and Surety. We no longer have to earn God's blessings through our own efforts because Christ has earned our blessings for us but the devil doesn't like that so he'll try to distract you from receiving your blessings. He'll try to steer your attention away from God through sin, guilt, condemnation, fear, servitude, human logic, etc. He'll try to make you earn your blessings although Christ has already earned them for you. That's why you need to renew your mind and fellowship with God daily so you can stay sharp and sensitive to the spirit of God.

Greater Blessings Defined

The term "blessings" in the context of this book is defined as "a favor or gift bestowed by God that brings happiness" or simply "a thing conducive to happiness or welfare." There are different categories or levels of blessings. The first category of blessing is the most common but people operating at this level don't have much control over what happens to them; things just happen when they do. For example, God created everybody to have antibodies and natural healing processes so when they get sick, they can rely on the natural healing process. At this level, the blessings of God seem natural, even to an unbeliever. Matthew 5:45 says God sends His rain and sun to the righteous as well as to the unrighteous so, even an unbeliever can benefit from God's blessings at this level. God is good and His goodness spills over to His entire creation; He extends His breadth of life to everyone and He allows all His creation to benefit from His laws of nature; laws of harvest, laws of reproduction, laws of gravity, laws of science, etc. At this level, people relate with God as master and they can only receive the crumps that fall off the table. When they are in trouble, they pray and hope that perhaps, God will do something. When they are sick and they get healed, it's only for a short while until next flu season. Every breakthrough comes through much struggle. At this level, you need to fast and pray for so long before you can get the smallest breakthrough and when the breakthrough occurs, it is short lived. God will still intervene but you would be vulnerable to the devil's schemes and natural chaos of this fallen world. You may still receive the benefits of your salvation but it will be with much struggle. When there's a prolonged crisis, those operating at this level tend to doubt the existence or power of God. You'll hear them say things like "does God really exist? Can He really hear me?" Some may become too dependent on the faith and anointing of others. They'll run to and fro searching for the latest man of God with the latest anointing in town because on their own, it's always a struggle. Christians operating at this level haven't grown into sonship. They're still babes that are easily swayed and tossed about by the chaos of life.

There is another category of blessings reserved only to sons and joint heirs with Christ. At this level, you have more control. You no longer relate with God as Master, but as Father. You are no longer a stranger but a son, a heir. Like Galatians 4:1 puts it, you are no longer a child tossed to and fro but you've grown to gain access to your inheritance. Jesus becomes more than Lord, He becomes your friend, your brother. You become family with God. You don't sit and wait for the next flu season because you have access to divine health. You don't wait for "luck", you make your way prosperous through the word of God in you. At this level, the blessings God has given you by promise now become accessible to you as your inheritance. Jesus said in John 17:22 *"And the glory which You gave Me I have given them, that they may be one just as We are one."* God would not share His glory with any idol but Jesus is saying here that He has shared His glory with you. That is what He wants. This is the level of friendship with God. It's a level of sonship. The greater blessings can only be accessed by sons; those who have grown to possess their inheritance in God. Apostle Peter is very bold in Acts 3:6. Instead of praying for a lame man, he says **"what I do have I give you:** *In the name of Jesus Christ of Nazareth, rise up and walk"*. He had gained possession of His inheritance. He said he had the power to heal the lame man. He wasn't just going to pray and hope that perhaps God will have mercy and heal. No! He healed that sick man. He possessed that power and he was aware it was his to use on whom ever he chose. When trouble comes your way, you don't just fall apart like an overused briefcase and wait for things to unfold naturally so that perhaps "luck" may smile on you. You use your inheritance. At this level, you can't be depressed. The way you pray changes. You don't say "God please let your presence come with us"; You say "Thank you Lord for your presence is here with us." You don't say "God please heal me"; you say "In the name of Jesus, I am healed." At this level, just like Joshua said in 1:8, you get to make your own way prosperous through your inheritance in Christ. This level of blessings is what this book refers to as "The Greater Blessings of God". It's not for everybody, it's for the household of God, for the family of God, for those who understand their sonship. If you've given your life to Christ and you are born again even if it was just seconds ago, you've been engrafted into the family of God. You are now a son but you need to grow and gain access to that sonship. It doesn't matter whether you are a clergy or just an ordinary believer. God wants you to operate at this level that is why God says; as He is, so are you in this world. Are you ready to walk in the greater blessings of God?

It is Finished- You are blessed

"And on the seventh day God ended His work which He had done, and He rested on the seventh day from all His work which He had done" –Genesis 2:2

In the beginning when God finished creating the universe, He rested. The Hebrew word used here isn't talking about resting because one is tired; it means to desist, cease or stop from doing something. Everything God had made was perfect; there was no need to create one more species, everything fit perfectly so God ceased from His work of creation but He was forced to go back to work when sin entered the world. However, in John 19:30, just before Jesus breathed His last, He repeated what He had said at creation. He said *"It is finished"*. The Greek word used here is *"teleó"* and it means "to *fulfill*", "to *accomplish*", *"to pay."* But what did He accomplish, fulfill or pay? Recall from chapter three that Jesus is the Surety of the New Covenant.

So Jesus fulfilled what was required of us to earn God's blessings by dying on the cross. God is not angry at you, He is not withholding His blessings from you because you have not prayed enough or because you are not holy. Jesus said *"It is finished"* so as Surety of the New Covenant, He has fulfilled our requirements. Hebrews 4:10 says *"For he who has entered His rest has himself also ceased from his works as God did from His."* Everything you need has already been made available for you so you too can rest and enjoy God's blessings the same way Adam freely enjoyed God's blessings prior to the fall.

In the Old Covenant, people had to earn their blessings. They had to obey every law and commandment for God to bless them. In the New Covenant, Jesus has fulfilled our requirements so all we need to do is accept His gift by faith and rest in His Grace. 2 Peter 1:3 says *"as His divine power* **has given to us all things** *that pertain to life and godliness…"* Ephesians 1:3 says *"Blessed be the God and Father of our Lord Jesus Christ, who* **has blessed us with every spiritual blessing** *in the heavenly places in Christ."* God has already made available for you every blessing you need. He is not going to bless you now because you asked Him, He's already blessed you. It's a done deal! Everything you need that pertains to life be it prosperity, happiness, joy, peace, healing, a spouse, a job, an education, success in business, wisdom, everything that constitutes life, God has already given you. In the same way, everything that constitutes your spirituality, be it anointing, growth in ministry, deeper experience of God's love, whatsoever it may be, God has already given you as well. When you know God has already blessed you, receiving it will be swifter than thinking He will manufacture the blessing at His will when you fulfill a certain requirement or wait for a period of time or fast and pray for a certain amount of time. God isn't asking you to wait because He's already given you the blessings you need. The wait period in receiving your blessings now depends on you.

God is Pleased to Bless You!

"Now I say that the heir, as long as he is a child, does not differ at all from a slave, though he is master of all, but is under guardians and stewards until the time appointed by the father. Even so we, when we were children, were in bondage under the elements of the world. But when the fullness of the time had come, God sent forth His Son, born of a woman, born under the law, to redeem those who were under the law, that we might receive the adoption as sons. And because you are sons, God has sent forth the Spirit of His Son into your hearts, crying out, "Abba, Father!" **Therefore you are no longer a slave but a son, and if a son, then an heir of God through Christ."***-*Galatians 4:1-7

God is pleased to bless you. The bible says He will not withhold any good thing from you[2]. You are no longer a slave but a son and daughter of God. You are God's heir. Jesus calls you son of God and He says God the father is delighted to give you the kingdom[3] and everything that is His. We've seen in chapter four how God loves you because He is love not because you are lovely. He created you for His pleasure and He delights in you. As a child and heir of God, it's your

---

God-given right to be blessed. It's your God-given right to be joyful, to be in good health, and to be prosperous - not because you are special by yourself but because Jesus made you special by Grace through faith. But if you remain a child (meaning ignorant, weak-willed, irresponsible in the things of God), the devil will toss you any way he wants and although you are a heir of God; although you now have authority over the devil and all his demons[4], if you remain a child and ignorant of your identity in Christ, Satan will torment you and deprive you of your inheritance. The devil will try to stop you from experiencing God's blessings through guilt and condemnation. He will try to convince you to earn your blessings and he'll cause you to doubt your worth. Your sins and imperfections does not stop God from blessing you because He has already blessed you. Galatians 3:5-10 says;

*"Answer this question: Does the God who lavishly provides you with his own presence, his Holy Spirit, working things in your lives you could never do for yourselves, **does he do these things because of your strenuous moral striving or because you trust him to do them in you?** Don't these things happen among you just as they happened with Abraham? He believed God, and that act of belief was turned into a life that was right with God"*-MSG

As the Surety of the New Covenant, God held Jesus responsible for fulfilling our requirements. The devil's tactics are meant to separate you from your blessings that is why the earlier chapters talked a lot about the Old and New Covenants so you would be aware of who you

---

[4] *Luke 10:19; Mark 16:17-18*

are in Christ. The devil will tell you "God killed your loved ones to teach you something" or "God caused you to go through a hardship to chastise and correct you." But that's not what the bible says. God is not the one who caused your loved ones to die and He doesn't cause you to go through hardships or crisis just so He can teach you a lesson. The devil is an evil devil and he seeks to hurt and steal from you. If you let the devil sow seeds of doubt, unbelief, fear, guilt and condemnation in your heart, he'll steal from you. If you let the devil succeed in turning your expectations away from the blessings and intent of God, he would have succeeded in stopping God's blessings in your life. No matter how much you pray or plead, you won't really experience God's greater blessings because you would have bought into the devil's deception. Proverbs 23:18-19 says;

"For surely there is a hereafter, And your hope will not be cut off. Hear, my son, and be wise; And guide your heart in the way."

This scripture is saying be wise and guide your heart for surely there is a hereafter; your hope, expectation shall not be cut off. Proverbs 13:12 says *"Hope deferred makes the heart sick"*. When you need a blessing and the devil tells you God is the one causing you to go through a crisis because He wants to teach you something, he's trying to redirect your expectation from God. He's trying to defer your hope. He's trying to steal from you. He's trying to tell you *"no need to pray because God is the cause"*. He's trying to tell you *"God can't bless you because you are not holy"*, *"you haven't prayed or fasted enough"*, *"your prayers are hindered"*, etc. The bible says it is the goodness of God that leads to repentance, not His wrath. If God needs to teach you something, He'll chastise you through His word[5] and through His goodness[6]. The bible teaches us to do good to our enemies because our acts of kindness are like heaping burning coals on their head[7]. If your short-comings separated you from God, don't you think God will at least abide by His own instructions to us and correct us through goodness and not wrath? God is just and will not command us to do something that He Himself would not do[8]. Amen!

Receive Your Blessing

Several months ago, I ordered a package from Amazon. However, I didn't receive it on the day it was supposed to be delivered so I called Amazon's customer service and they informed me their tracking information showed my package had been delivered. They called the shipper who confirmed my package was left at the right address but I had not physically gained possession of the package. A few days later, my neighbor knocked at my door and informed me she'd kept my package because I wasn't home at the time the package was being delivered. So, my package was delivered to the right address, but it was my responsibility to be at home to receive it. In the same way, God has given us His blessings and they have already been delivered however, the responsibility of physically gaining possession of them is ours. My neighbor was kind enough to keep my package safe. The devil on the

---

[5] 2 Timothy 3:16
[6] Romans 2:4
[7] Romans 12:20, Proverbs 25:21-22
[8] Hebrews 2:17

other hand is not so kind; he won't keep your package safe. You have to know how to receive it yourself.

The three steps for physically gaining possession and walking in the greater blessings are Knowing the giver (God), Acknowledging what He has already given you (His gifts and blessings that are already in you) and Receiving your inheritance by Grace through Faith (K.A.F).

Knowing the Giver (K)

*"Grace and peace be multiplied to you **in the knowledge of God and of Jesus** our Lord as His divine power has given to us all things that pertain to life and godliness, **through the knowledge of Him** who called us by glory and virtue"* -2Peter 1:2-3

The first step of receiving God's greater blessings is having a working knowledge of who the giver is. You need to experientially know who God is, His attributes and how He gives. It's through the knowledge of Him that you can receive His greater blessings.

The Greek word for "knowledge" in this scripture is *"epignóseos"*. It is used here as a genitive noun (N-GFS)[9] of the Greek word *"epignósis"* and it means precise and complete knowledge or awareness of the nature and benefits of God, gained through a first-hand relationship. The Amplified Bible Classic edition (AMPC) puts it this way:

---

[9] *Genitive Feminine singular noun*

*"For His divine power has bestowed upon us all things that [are requisite and suited] to life and godliness, through the **[full, personal] knowledge of Him** Who called us by and to His own glory and excellence (virtue)"* -2Peter 1:3

This is not knowledge gained merely from research or studying. It's not second hand knowledge, but personal, experiential knowledge of God. This is not just information gotten through the pages of the bible or from a preacher. James 2:19 says even demons believe there is one God and tremble yet demons cannot have faith in God; they cannot receive God's blessings despite their knowledge of God. 2Corinthians 3:6 says the letter kills but the spirit gives life. The Greek words for "kill" and "letter" in this scripture are "*apokteinō*" and "*gramma*" respectively. *Apokteinō* means to deprive of spiritual life and *gramma* means written document such as a letter or an epistle. This is basically saying the written letters of the bible doesn't possess any power in itself to edify any one that reads it. So, the knowledge that would grant you access to the greater blessings is not merely reading about God from the pages of the bible. Studying the bible and knowing what it says is important but you shouldn't stop at that level. You need to go a notch higher in your quest of knowing God the giver. You need to let the Spirit of God make this knowledge come alive in you. Jesus said in John 6:63 "*It is the Spirit who gives life; the flesh profits nothing. The words that I speak to you are spirit, and they are life*". John 16:13 says the Holy Spirit will not speak of His own but He will speak what He hears (from Jesus). This is what gives life to the letter of the pages of the bible – the Spirit of Truth. You may have gained knowledge about God from a preacher, your personal research or even through this book, but you need to experience God personally through the knowledge you received by letting the Holy Spirit quicken the word of God and make it come alive in you. This level of knowledge can only come through an active relationship with the Holy Spirit. As your teacher, the Holy Spirit wants to personally teach you who God is and what the attributes of His divine nature are. By praying in tongues, a Christian is speaking mysteries in the Spirit[10]. The Holy Spirit reveals these mysteries to us[11]. However, these mysteries are not some strange information from space. The bible says cursed in anyone who adds or subtracts anything from the scriptures[12] so the Holy Spirit won't give you any new knowledge that is not in scriptures however, He'll make the scriptures come alive in you as you pray in tongues and fellowship with Him. He will give you a divine understanding of the scriptures and will cause you to experience this knowledge spiritually. It will become your personal experiential knowledge of what is written in the scriptures. You'll become a living testament of the scriptures.

In 2Peter 1:3, knowledge is used in the genitive case which is a possessive noun. So, this is a knowledge you've possessed and made your own through the Holy Spirit. When you study the word of God or research about the things of God, you need to let the Holy Spirit transform that knowledge and make it your own. So, it changes from "this person said this about God" or "this book said this about God"

---

[10] *1Corinthians 14:2*
[11] *1corinthians 2:2-16; Colossians 1:26; Ephesians 1:9; Ephesians 3:4-6; Matthew 13:11*
[12] *Deuteronomy 4:2; 12:32; Revelations 22:18-19; Proverbs 30:5-6*

to "the Holy Spirit revealed this to me through this book or through this preacher." Do you see the difference? The former is just information you read or heard from someone and you may not even know for sure how it works but the latter is knowledge that you've personally experienced in the Spirit and it's now become your own. You may have gotten it originally from someone but the Holy Spirit has made it yours by personally telling you how it works and you get to experience this knowledge for yourself. 2Peter 1:3 says it's through your experiential knowledge of God that you receive everything that pertains to life and godliness.

God's blessings are not meant only for a certain group of people; they are meant for all born again believers; novice or mature, clergy or ordinary Joe Blow believer. An average Christian has the power to raise the dead and heal the sick and perform miracles residing inside him/her. As a family of God, we should lean on one another for strength and mutual growth but we need to realize that God's blessings are meant for all His children and you can receive it directly. In times when you are weak, I encourage you to lean on a man of God, or a brother or sister in the Lord who has the gifts you need, just long enough to get a "jumpstart" or to get back on your feet. A car cannot run on a jump-starter so once you are strong, rise up and assist another person. Don't rely on someone else for all your spiritual needs because God wants to bless you so that when you are strong enough, you can bless others. Psalm 82:6-7 says;

*"I said, "***You are gods** *and all of you are children of the Most High.* **But you shall die like men***, and fall like one of the princes."*

Ecclesiastes 10:6-7 says "Folly is set in great dignity, while the rich sit in a lowly place. I have seen servants on horses, while princes walk on the ground like servants."

As a heir, son/daughter and prince of God, God is raising you to execute His standards on earth and He has blessed you tremendously so you can become a blessing to your neighbor. The same power that raised Christ from the dead resides inside you but if you are ignorant of who you are in Christ and who God is to you, the devil will steal from you. Although you are a prince and priest of the Most High, and a heir and son of God, you will beg like a slave, you will eat the crumps on the floor like a dog although you are a son. If you aren't aware of who you are in Christ, you shall die like a mere mortal although you have the Spirit of God residing on the inside of you. This is a great folly. Don't let this happen. Take your place in God!

Acknowledge His gift(s) in you (A)

"That the sharing of your faith may become effective **by the acknowledgment of every good thing which is in you** *in Christ Jesus." - Philemon 1:6*

The second step is to acknowledge the blessings God has already reserved for you. The Greek word for "acknowledge" in this scripture is *"epignosei"* which is used a dative noun (N-DFS)[13] of the Greek word

---

[13] *Dative Feminine Singular Noun*

"*epignόsis*" and it means precise and complete knowledge of a thing known. This is referring to having a complete and accurate knowledge of the blessings God has already made available for you. This too is referring to personal knowledge gotten through first-hand relationship with God. The Amplified Version puts it this way:

"I pray that the sharing of your faith may become effective and powerful because of ***your accurate knowledge of every good thing which is ours*** *in Christ"–Philemon 6*

If you know that peace is the fruit of the Spirit and it's already in you but you don't concede, or admit, or accept, or allow this truth to operate in your life for whatever reason, you've known about it, but it hasn't yet become a personal first-hand knowledge. For example, you know the bible says promotion comes from the Lord. But when you need a promotion, you try to cheat your way up. Maybe you slander a coworker or use tricks to move your way up. You've known about the blessing but you haven't acknowledged it. No matter how much you fast and pray, you won't experience this blessing because you haven't conceded to it. You haven't allowed it to run its full course in your life. You may still get the promotion, but it would be by your efforts, not God's blessing. In this example, if you paved your own way, it will take your own efforts to maintain that promotion not God's grace. If you need growth in your ministry, you need to experientially know and acknowledge both God and everything He has already blessed you with that pertains to life and godliness. You can ask God for wisdom on how to manifest these blessings but unless you acknowledge what they are, your faith for receiving them cannot become effective. 1Corinthians 2:12 says;

*"Now we have received, not the spirit of the world, but the **Spirit who is from God, that we might know the things that have been freely given to us by God***"

When the devil or our fallen world throws sickness at you, you can overcome and live healthy; When your bank account sends you a "note" that says you are broke, you can overcome and prosper supernaturally. When depression or anxiety knocks at your door, you can overcome and not let it come near you. Paul is saying in 1Corinthians 2 that God has freely blessed us and the Spirit of God will make us aware of these gifts. These are not mere blessings, they are the greater blessings reserved for sons. This is the kind of blessing that enabled Apostle Peter and John to heal the lame man at the temple in Acts 3. This is the kind of blessing that made Apostle Paul raise Eutychus from the dead in Acts 20. The greater blessings made Jesus calm the tempest and called Peter to walk on water. They didn't pray and say "God please heal the sick" or please "calm the storm". They already had that power operation them. They had grown to sonship and had access to their inheritance in Christ. Yes, study the bible and research what these gifts that are already in you through Christ are, but it's the Holy Spirit who will activate this knowledge and make it come alive in you. As you fellowship with the Holy Spirit, He will transform this knowledge and make it a personal experiential knowledge.

Apostle Paul and Timothy are both saying in Philemon 1:6 that your faith becomes effective by acknowledging what is already in you in Christ. Amen!

Grace through Faith (F)

Everything you received from God was given to you by Grace. You can't deserve it. You can't work for it or earn it. Jesus worked and earned it for you so all you need to do is receive it freely, as an undeserved gift. God won't force anything on you. He gives His blessings by Grace, but you have a responsibility of receiving it by faith. Grace works through Faith[14] and Faith works by love[15]. The bible is not obsolete and God has not changed. You can rely on His Word. Study the word of God to build-up your faith. Fellowship with the God to "sharpen" your senses to the Spirit of God[16]. Pray and meditate on God's word to sharpen your senses to God so you can receive the epignósis of Him and the gifts He has reserved for you.

While growing up, I had a severe asthma which usually made it hard to breathe. Breathing became more and more strenuous and my lungs began to hurt so much that I wished I would die. The inhaler my doctor prescribed wasn't effective anymore so I needed a different dosage but I knew I didn't want to rely on medications for the rest of my life; I wanted to live freely. I needed a blessing and I never wanted to feel sick again. So, I studied the scriptures and found God's

---

[14] *Ephesians 2:8*
[15] *Galatians 5:6*
[16] *Proverbs 27:17*

promises regarding my situation; the bible says He sent His word and **healed** my diseases. By His stripes I **was healed**. These signs shall follow them that believe… they shall lay hands on the sick and they shall recover. I was still learning these truths so it was a struggle but I was learning fast. I became so immersed in these scriptures that they became more than mere words on a piece of paper. God made it real to me. It became a direct word from God to me. Many times I would hear the Holy Spirit whisper the words that I read back to my heart. Then I began to acknowledge these promises as truth. Although I was physically sick, I knew the real me is spirit and God's blessings reside in my spirit. I couldn't see it but I acknowledged that it was absolute truth and it was meant for me; I needed the blessings in my physical body and that's where faith came in. When I prayed, my faith prevailed because I knew God wanted me well. I knew God is a good God and He wasn't responsible for my sickness. I knew God didn't want me to work for or earn my healing but He wanted me to just believe in my heart and confess with my mouth what His word says. So, I acknowledged His promises regarding my health. I started to release words of faith. I said *"In the name of Jesus, I am healed, in the name of Jesus I command this asthma to cease."* I would lay my own hands on my head and command the sickness to leave. I was no longer praying to God to heal me but I was commanding the sickness to leave. I had gained epignósis of who God was, His nature, His intent and the blessings He'd already made available for me. It took some patience but I had known the truth and I clung to it like glue. Some times when I laid my hands on my head and prayed, I would receive instant relief.

Sometimes it took hours of praying and I will just get tired then I would fall asleep. Gradually, I began to understand this principle and the process became easier and easier until one day I declared "*Asthma, you have no place in my body. I command you right now to leave and never return.*" That was it! I was delivered. It's been more than 14 years today and I've never been sick of anything, not even a cold or flu. I don't know what flu season feels like because I don't suffer from it any more. A few months ago, my military dentist recommended that I remove all my molars in order to prevent future infections. If you are familiar with the way the military works you'd know there's really no such thing as "it's highly recommended". It's more like a command so I had to do it. After taking out my molars, the dentist gave me some pain killers but I never got to use them. A few hours later, after the effects of the numbness ceased, I was eating like nothing had happened. I didn't have to use the pain killers because I didn't need to. One of my buddies who had his molars removed as well was shoving pain killers through his mouth like candy but I knew the Holy Spirit had revitalized my mortal body[17] and I didn't have a need for the pain killers. It's not wrong to take pain killers, but I didn't need them because the Holy Spirit supernaturally caused my pain to subside.

When my daughter was a little over a year old, she always came back from the day care with the flu and wouldn't sleep all night despite taking all her immunization shots. So, I decided to exercise my authority as a co-heir with Christ. My wife and I laid our hands on our

---

[17] *Romans 8:11*

daughter and healed her. We also proclaimed that she would be immune to the flu virus. She still goes to the same daycare and even when her friends have the flu, she doesn't anymore. I have many more examples of how I've applied these principle in many other areas of my life that I could write an entire book just narrating testimony after testimony. I am seeing God's greater blessings in my finances, education, marriage, ministry, relationships and even my military service and I can attest that it works. As a co-heir with Christ, you can have a say in how you respond to what happens to and around you. You are a solution to the world's crisis. This is the realm of the greater blessings, Amen!

I've seen God come through for me supernaturally, over and over. It's no longer knowledge that I read in a book or from the pages of the bible. It's now an experiential knowledge that is far superior to any argument. When everyone is saying there's a casting down, you can say there's a lifting up. When everyone is saying the economy is going down, you can say your finances are going up. When there's a reason to be sad, you can say the joy of the Lord is your strength. Sadness, depression, anxiety won't be a part of you anymore because the fruit of the spirit would be working inside of you.

Our fallen world would try to be a hindrance, the devil too will come at you so don't be ignorant of his schemes. Fellowship with God through His word and prayer because He loves you. Meditate on and study the word of God and acknowledge what it says to build your faith and your life will never be the same again. Amen!

CHAPTER SEVEN
ENCOURAGE YOURSELF IN THE LORD

When things get tough and you see no way out, just like David did, strengthen yourself in the lord. Learn to edify yourself in God. Even if no one commends you; even if no one encourages or acknowledges you, learn to acknowledge yourself. Learn to encourage yourself! The word of God is not burdensome because we were born of it. We never consider it a burdensome task to breathe (unless we have a disease or ailment) or desire a break from breathing even though we breathe every second of our lives because we were designed to breathe on land but a fish can't breathe out of water; it will die. As a born again Christian, God made you to be, do and live according to His Word, that's why He says we shall not live by bread alone but by every Word of God[1] meaning that we shall not live on the things that gratify the flesh but on the word of God which is the food of the spirit. You just need to make the word of God your way of life until you are wholly conformed to it. Apostle Paul commended the church in Corinth in 2Corinthians 3:2-3 saying;

"You are our epistle written in our hearts, known and read by all men; clearly you are an epistle of Christ, ministered by us, written not with ink but by the Spirit of the living God, not on tablets of stone but on tablets of flesh, that is, of the heart."
According to Apostle Paul, the Church in Corinth was an epistle of Christ which they ministered. But Paul said in 1Corinthians 1:23 that

---

[1] *Deuteronomy 8:3, Matthew 4:4*

he preached Christ crucified. Combining both scriptures, Paul was saying that the believers in Corinth were so conformed to the word of God that preaching the gospel of Christ was like preaching about them; their lives were an epistle of Christ crucified. Although the Church in Corinth had their issues and at one time were very ungodly, the bible says they repented[2] and were now conformed to God's word to the point where Apostle Paul said they (their way of life) were an epistle of Christ. Let the word of God sink into your heart in like manner.

It Comes with The Package!

When I was much younger my father shared an inspiring story with me through which I've gained a lot of life lessons so, I'd like to share it with you as well.

Once upon a time many years ago before modern technology lived a young man who wanted to travel overseas to search for greener pastures but he couldn't afford a plane ticket so he decided to go by sea. He sold everything he had and worked hard to raise some money for his trip. After paying for his ticket, seeing that he did not have much money left for food and other basic expenses, he bought some snacks which is what he ate throughout the voyage. Many times during the journey, he starved and regretted boarding that ship but it was too late; they were now far from shore and he couldn't swim back to land. Several weeks later, they arrived at their destination and after everybody had alighted, a kind hostess accosted him and asked politely

---

[2] *2 Corinthians 7:8-11*

"sir, I noticed that throughout the journey, you didn't eat our food rather you slept with the ship laborers in the lower compartment....You looked miserable and disapproving of our services. Did we do anything wrong?" The man now puzzled, said *"are you kidding? I could neither afford your luxurious rooms nor your food. They were just too expensive for me."* Then the hostess after taking a quick look at the man's ticket said *"Sir, you've got a premium ticket that entitled you to food, lodging in one of our best suites and other amenities."* Well, you can imagine the look on this man's face after hearing this. What do you think his problem was? He had been too concerned about making his trip that he spent much time and effort looking for money but when he got it, he did not realize the comfort the money he had amassed could give him. He had a knowledge problem. This is the same reason many Christians fail to possess their spiritual inheritance. Acts 20:32 says the word of God is able to build you up and give you an inheritance. The same way the man in this story was ignorant of the privileges and comfort he already had access to through his premium ticket, believers too will discover at the end of their journey in heaven before the throne of God that they had access to the fullness of God but didn't make use of it. Revelations 7:17 says God will wipe our teas away. We'll realize how much of God's grace and goodness was available for us but we failed to appropriate them. God has already paid the full price for you to enjoy. 1Corinthians 3:21 says; *"Therefore let no one boast in men. For all things are yours"*

Psalm 35:27 says; *"Let the Lord be magnified, Who has pleasure in the prosperity of His servant."*

Isaiah 53:5 says *"But He was wounded for our transgressions, He was bruised for our iniquities; The chastisement for our peace was upon Him, And by His stripes we are healed."*

Did you know healing is an integral part of your "premium salvation ticket"? If you can be born again, then you can also be healed of your ailments. It's all bundled up in your "Salvation ticket"

Psalm 34:10 says; *"The young lions lack and suffer hunger; But those who seek the Lord shall not lack any good thing."*

Every good and perfect gift comes from God[3]. He doesn't want you to lack any good thing. If it is good, God wants you to have it. It's all bundled-up in your "premium salvation ticket" the moment you got born again. What will you do with it? Chill with the laborers at the lower compartment or enjoy all the amenities you now have access to?

The devil is a bad devil and he is out to steal, kill, and destroy. He is the cause of deaths, sickness, sorrow and every bad thing. James 1:17 says; *"Every good gift and every perfect gift is from above, and comes down from the Father of lights, with whom there is no variation or shadow of turning."* God is a good God in every meaning of the word. If you believe in Jesus, you are no longer subject to Satan. Jesus said Satan has nothing in Him and we are hid in Christ in God[4]. Amen!

Assurance in His word

In times when things don't go your way, when there seems to be

---

[3] James 1:17
[4] John 14:30; Colossians 3:3

a prolonged wait in seeing God's greater blessings tangibly evident in your life, don't be discouraged and don't think God does not care. God cares; His love for you is unconditional and eternal. He will always love you and His word is your sure assurance. Galatians 6:9 says *"And let us not grow weary while doing good, for in due season we shall reap if we do not lose heart"*. Don't lose heart, hang on!

John the Baptist testified of Jesus that He was the Christ. When he was put in prison and he saw that Herod would soon behead him, he was troubled. He sent his disciples to Jesus to ask if He was really the Christ. In other words, the things John the Baptist was going through weighed down on him to the extent that he began to doubt the very words the Spirit of God had spoken through him about Jesus. He began to doubt the Holy Spirit who had testified through him that Jesus was the Messiah even though he'd seen the Holy Spirit descend on Jesus like a dove and even though he'd heard God's voice loud and clear when He said *"This is my beloved Son in whom I'm well pleased."* In time of prolonged trouble, John began to doubt everything he'd seen and heard about Jesus. His whole life now seemed to be a lie; his purpose, the reason he was born, all the strict and regimented lifestyle he had lived, everything seemed to be falling apart.

When in a prolonged crisis, some people tend to doubt God even though at some point in the past they might have been so certain they'd heard from God. In the past, you might have received a miracle or a word of prophecy or a divine instruction or just an inspiring word from scripture. At the time you received it, you might have been so sure that it was from God. But some time later, when things didn't go as planned; maybe the miracle was short lived, maybe the promise was delayed, maybe everything began to go contrary to the prophecy or word you'd heard from God; you might be discouraged and doubt. John the Baptist was going through a very similar situation. When he sent his disciples to ask Jesus if he was indeed the Christ, Jesus did not answer John's disciples directly by telling them plainly who He was. Rather, He gave them the scriptures[5]. Jesus fulfilled and quoted Isaiah 35:5-6; 61:1 to John's disciples because these scriptures were talking about who the Christ was and John the Baptist was very versed with them. Jesus wanted John to know Him based on what the scriptures say not based on sight or emotions or what the physical senses say. God wants you to know Him by faith not by sight. He does not want you to relate with Him based on your sensual feelings but based on faith (which most often contradicts the carnal order of things) which is built through the word of God.

There was a time in my life, about a decade ago where my family and I were going through some real tough financial and emotional hardships. My world was falling apart and I had no hope for the future. Things were so tough, I lost my desire to live. I knew what the scriptures say but like John the Baptist, I started to lose faith in God's word. Like Elijah, I'd started to entertain doubts in my mind because I felt like I was at the end of my rope. At the time, God had just started teaching me the revelation about how to receive His greater blessings

---

[5] Matthew 11:3-6

but I was still struggling. My life became too uncomfortable to live. I asked God countless times what the issue was but He always said to me every time I asked, that everything was alright and that He **had** blessed me but there was no correlation with what God said and what I was going through. Now I understand what God meant. God was reminding me of the scriptures the same way He did to John the Baptist. Ephesians 1:3-4 says:

*"Blessed be the God and Father of our Lord Jesus Christ, **who has blessed us** with every spiritual blessing in the heavenly places in Christ."*

2 Peter 1:3 says it's through the knowledge of God that you can get the blessing of God to manifest in my life. It is your responsibility to build your faith in His word until it becomes physically tangible in your life. Sometimes, when we face trials and adversities, we are quick to let the devil build fear and unbelief in our minds instead of letting the word of God build faith in us. I have been to so many churches and I've seen Christians flood the pews at prayer meetings in search of a quick "Band-Aid" prayer but these same Christians ignore bible study meetings. Some Bible study meetings tend to be so empty, you could hear a pin drop. The right kind of prayer is important and knowledge of the word of God is imperative as well. Psalm 183:2 says *"For You have magnified Your word above all Your name."* The word of God is important, very important. That is why Apostle Paul's farewell message to the Ephesians in Acts 20:32 was;

"I commend you to God and to the word of His grace, which is able to build you up and give you an inheritance among all those who are sanctified."

Praying is good but what will build you up as a son and joint heir with Christ, and give you access to your inheritance and the greater blessings in this life is the word of God. Rather than giving-in to depression or sadness, complaining and saying, *"it is natural to feel this way"* (thereby making you natural/carnal instead of Spiritual), speak the word of God. Say "I *am prosperous in Christ"*, *"I am delivered"*, *"I am healed"*, *"I am the righteousness of God in Christ Jesus"*, *"God loves me dearly"*, *"I am blessed beyond the curse"*, *"I am a king and priest of the most high"*, *"I reign in life through Christ"*, *"I am a heir of God and joint heir with Christ"*, *"Jesus is my brother and friend"*, *"The most high God knows my name for I'm inscribed on the palms of His hands"*, *"God is excited about me"*, *"the joy of the lord is my strength"*, *"God does not withhold any good thing from me"*. The Holy Spirit will bear witness in your heart as you proclaim who you are in Christ and what He's already deposited in you. Before you know it, faith would swell up in you like a giant. Don't just confess these things with your mouth but also have an absolute assurance in your heart about what you confess. Have an experiential knowledge of God's word to the extent that even if the promises seem to delay, you'd still know that they are true and you'll not lose faith. Shadrach, Meshach, and Abed-nego said God was able to deliver them from the fiery furnace but even if He didn't save them, they'd still refuse to bow to an idol. That is the language of a renewed mind; a mind that knows God. Those who know their God will be strong and do great exploits[6]. 1Corinthians 4:20 says:

"For the kingdom of God is not in word but in power."

---

[6] *Daniel 11:32*

2Timothy 3:5 says *"…having a form of godliness but denying its power. And from such people turn away!"*

Christianity isn't just some guidelines for morality. It's not just going to church and looking pretty. True Christianity is a relationship with God that births in us power to bring supernatural change in our everyday lives. Paul says turn away from people who may appear to be moral or godly yet refuse the power that comes with it. Do you want positive, supernatural change in your life or situation? Fellowship with the word of God with a renewed mind. With your mouth and mind, profess the word of God and with faith and understanding in your heart believe what the word of God says until it becomes evident in your life. God's word is ultimate and it overrules our personal opinions and experiences. Therefore, be encouraged in the Lord and grow in His might as your mind is renewed day by day in the Holy Spirit. Amen!

Only a person who has been born again can have access to the greater blessings of God because the things of God are spiritually discerned. Hell is real but God wants to save you not only from Hell, but also from the struggles and hopelessness of this life. He wants you to experience His grace in this life and the next. Yes, you can live the higher life through Christ. You need God in your life! Having a real relationship with God is truly amazing! God so loved you that He let His son whom He loved dearly, die for you. The value of a thing is determined by what people are willing to pay for it. At what price were you bought? What's your value? 1Peter 1:19 says *"For you know what was paid to set you free from the worthless manner of life handed down by your ancestors.*

It was not something that can be destroyed, such as silver or gold; it was the costly sacrifice of Christ, who was like a lamb without defect or flaw." -TEV

We know God values us exceedingly to the extent that He didn't mind laying down His life for us. To God, your life is worth the very life of Jesus[7]. Despite His pure love for us, we disobeyed our creator and we deserved to be punished a thousand times over but Jesus took our punishment by dying on the cross so we could be saved. If you don't have an intimate relationship with Jesus or if you are not born again, I encourage you to consider receiving Jesus in your life and be born again so that you may begin to rediscover a new life in Christ Jesus. What is required of you is to confess Jesus with your mouth and believe in your heart that Jesus died for your sins and rose up again so that you might reign with Him. Pray a sincere prayer to profess your desire for God and your life will never be the same gain.

If you are already born again, pray that the Holy Spirit strengthens you with might in your inner man as He leads your heart to all truths. Amen!

If you have any requests, a story to share, a testimony or if you would like to stay connected, please reach out to my team through email at newnessoflifeseries@outlook.com

You are Blessed!

---

[7] *Acts 20:28, 1Corinthians 6:19-20; 7:23, Titus 2:14, 1Peter 1:18-19, Hebrews 9:12, Revelations 5:9,*

BIBLIOGRAPHY

Gesenius, Wilhelm, et al. *The Brown-Driver-Briggs Lexicon: with an Appendix Containing the Biblical Aramaic, Coded with the Numbering System from Strongs Exhaustive Concordance of the Bible Based on the Lexicon of William Gesenius as Translated by Edward Robinson.* Hendrickson, 1996

Thayer, Joseph Henry., et al. *Greek-English Lexicon of the New Testament: Being Grimms Wilkes Clavis Novi Testamenti.* Hendrickson Pub., 1999.

Index

ABOUT THE AUTHOR

In June 1998, E N Jinor had an extraordinary encounter with the Holy Spirit that transformed his life. Since then he's taught the unconditional Love and Grace of God. By the Grace of God and through his walk with the Holy Spirit, E N Jinor has experienced the tangible power of God in and through Him. His passion is in helping Christians grow in their walk of faith and fully reaching their potential in Christ.

E N Jinor has led prayer cell groups and was also a leader at a national non-denominational campus fellowship in Cameroon. He now resides in North Dakota with his family where he continues to teach the unconditional Love and Grace of God.

NOTES

21931119R00095

Made in the USA
Columbia, SC
23 July 2018